THE 20TH CENTURY'S TIME STATUE HARVEST

Robert F. Morgan

Morgan Foundation Publishers. Email:
morganfoundation@earthlink.net

ISBN: 978-1-885679-37-6 paperback

Web page:
htpp://www.morganfoundationpublishers.com

THE 20TH CENTURY'S TIME STATUE HARVEST

Robert F. Morgan

NOTE: Cover Photos include Becky Owl (left bottom) with unidentified male victim in the late 1970s at the University of Montana, and Becky Owl Morgan (right bottom) at *Fuddruckers* more recently.

CONTENTS

Dedication

Theme: *Here Comes the Sun* George Harrison

According to DNA analysis, about 160,000 years ago there was a mother in East Africa who had many children. There were other families living there and then. Yet it was her children that survived to spread through the earth. Through the millennia, to become the human family of today.

Shaped in appearance by different surroundings, shaped in action by diversity in culture and its gifts. The 2st century opportunity is to bring all these cultural gifts together, home. The Olympics begin this for athletics. Much more is possible.

On a much smaller scale, this book harvests some of our most glowing time statues from recent print along with new ones. Our East African mother's descendants are all our cousins. For them, all now in our temporal geography, what follows is written for them.

CREATIVITY
IS INTELLIGENCE
HAVING FUN.
ALBERT EINSTEIN

Time Statue Harvest:
20ᵗʰ Century

Themes: *We are Family* Sister Sledge; *Reunion* Bobbie Gentry; *Sing Our Own Song* Buffy Sainte- Marie; *The Good, the Bad, and the Ugly* Danish National Symphony Orchestra; *Walk on the Wild Side instrumental* Jimmy Smith; *Time Will Tell (theme from The Wizards)* Susan Anton.

Time is a place. Every moment is a statue in time, always there in that time and place. Our life includes some that stand out, glow. In this book we harvest the ones from each of the last six decades of the 20ᵗʰ century. Many are new, some that fit best are recreated from earlier *Time Statue* books.

They were often recovered in dreams. Some in sleep, reliably every 90 minutes, some in that semi-wakeful twilight time between waking and getting up, some while daydreaming apart from whatever reality surrounds.

The book that follows this one will cover the more recent 21st century, so far.

She was the matriarch of a large family. Lived in an isolated region, inside a mountain top. When each of her children became an adult, they began the SEARCH. Gone for a year, off in a new direction, unknown territory. Most survived to come home when the year was up. To share what they had learned, what or who they brought back. These gifts were absorbed in the family, celebrated as due, for a restful year at home. Then, as the next year began, off again in a new direction. Searching for new treasures. Thanks to this SEARCH, they flourished. Not sure if they ever knew that they were living, on a much smaller scale, the best harvest of Earth cultures. One our entire human family was approaching.

DNA scientists discovered that all humans alive today can be traced to a mother about 160,000 years ago in East Africa. She lived near other human or humanoid families at the time. Yet over the eons, setting aside trace DNA of Neanderthal or other unique contributions, it was her children alone through their generations that survived, and thrived, to inhabit today's Earth. As our human family. Yes, across the Earth, we are all cousins.

Over this epic time, it is estimated that those born in one place died no farther than five miles away. Yet in 160,000 years they did eventually inhabit the planet. Even if we assume that about half of all these people each millennium died before reproducing. Died from various disasters from predators, climate, eruptions, flood, fires, and, of course, each other.

Isolated in pockets of the earth, survivor skills evolved into culture. Psychologist Art McDonald described best how their local environment shaped them. Eight hundred years in snow country and the skin was white. Eight hundred years in hot jungle required nocturnal living and the skin was black. In this way surviving enclaves developed through natural selection the best protective skin- red, gold, brown, black, white. McDonald brings in the weather, available food, epidemic resistance and much more. Where each colony lived, their surrounds remade them.

And their culture. Language, weapons, creations, traditions, art, music, ideas, insights, technologies, ways of living together, ways of living with the land. Progress forward.   In each of these separate cultures there were true gifts and some grave errors. What was missing was some way for each cultural pocket to connect with the others.

Now, in our modern era, we have seen transportation advances connect them, all over the globe. Meaning the DNA was mixing to more diverse and adaptive forms.

And then, we have seen a communication revolution, connecting us even more thoroughly. These both opened the doors to a powerful sharing of the gifts from every culture. The Olympics every few years, based only on athletics, is a beginning and a model for much more.

And, careful now, some cultural byproducts are not gifts. Including seeds of destruction- nuclear war, epidemics, monopolistic greed engendering an accelerating climate change on a path to a planet devoid of life.

Still, we now have the means to harvest the *best* of each cultural pocket, true fruits of 160,000 years of planetary dispersal. Bring them all home. We can do it *now*.

Gather in this harvest while time still allows it.

Introduction

Book Theme: *Time Will Tell* Susan Anton from the movie *Wizards*

Time is a place. Each moment is a statue in time, always rooted in that time and that place.

> *When I was five years old, my mother always told me that happiness was the key to life. When I went to school, they asked me what I wanted to be when I grew up. I wrote down 'happy.' They told me I didn't understand the assignment, and I told them they didn't understand life."*
>
> –John Lennon

> *"Because we are born for a brief span of life, and because this spell of time that has been given to us rushes so swiftly and rapidly that with very few exceptions life ceases for the rest of us just when we are getting ready for it. It is not that we have a short time to live, but that we waste a lot of it. Our lifetime extends amply if you manage it properly."*
>
> -Seneca, 65BCE, 2004 AD

After eight decades, I have amassed a library of memories. Stacks after stacks of time statues archives. So much that it can take minutes or more to access just one memory and only with patience. Elders do better at this when we imagine our search as an ordering at a restaurant. Then, usually, it will come.

Arriving late? But it will come.

From the viewpoint of age, we can view these memories in their entirety as a grand tapestry. What is a good guiding strategy for navigating these patterns, this treasure in an elder's experience? Maybe it's ones that were meaningful or fun. Sometimes both?

All of these can be shared.

Well, at least some statues in time can be worth a visit. Or, on reflection, a revisit.

"Peter Rabbit" was a children's play I took my daughters to when they were very young. Peter began each day with great joy for the inevitable adventure. A day for him seemed like a whole season for us humans.

Remember in our own childhood how the beginning of the summer vacation seemed like the opening of endless days? For the shorter lifespan rabbit, each day was like that. It was a revelation for me. A fresh approach.

Learning to perceive the *Umwelt* (world view) of animals has the added benefit of enhancing empathy for own species.

For one, humans have great individual variations of time perception. Working with older people, I often saw anxiety about how few years of life it seemed that they had left.

I had been working with the full spectrum of human aging and life extension experts, Jim Birren to Timothy Leary. They approached the subject with biology as cause and with psychology as consequence.

What if we reversed the order?

What if seniors with the life expectancy of less than a decade approached each day as a season in itself?

Instead of ten birthdays and out, why not 3,650 individual seasons to savor, one at a time?

To do this, the senior would need to slow the rocketing passage of time engendered by similar days. Magnified by retirement or illness, one day is much like another. They go by in a flash.

This may be comforting but life then goes by quickly. But if each day was differentiated as its own adventure, time will slow down. Life extension occurs experientially. For some, those who accomplished this, they said it helped very much.

We're not rabbits. We live much longer. Or so we can learn to do.

Can each of our days and the moments within them become simply statues of adventure in time?

Although many are protected by metaphorical police tape. Worth the trip?

Building on the five book series *"Time Statues Revisited"* and the follow-up *"Future Time Statues"*, once again we come to Einstein and Vonnegut: the temporal community is a place.

Each day we finish is fixed for all time. Or is it?

We can revisit, this time for new and more challenging ones.

This time we go to the even more interesting ones, in two newer *Time Statue Harvest* books. This 20th century one precedes the 21st century one that follows.

As we get older and remember our past, our regrets are more often what we did *not* do than what we did. Either way, a revisit to most interesting or surprising remote events seems worth the return trip.

Despite some statues best forgotten.

To navigate effectively in our own normal environment, it is entirely reasonable to consider time as linear and irreversible.

A nonlinear approach will naturally unearth exceptions.

The passage through time carries us forward, evolving and adapting.

In our nonlinear world, if we are open to it, we can find ways to detour against the current as part of our healthy development.

It makes for a richer tapestry than had been expected.

To help, each chapter begins with a link to a musical theme.

Each moment we live includes our action as our art. Good art or bad art, all that we do sculpts a second-by-second statue to inhabit that time and that place.

The artist continues to live in the limited moments of this lifespan community.

Yet the consequences of this art can travel ever further, transcending dangers and obstacles, to shape a better future for our human community.

In this way, we can too.

Optional Music Themes

Theme: *Put another Nickel* in Teresa Brewer

Just below the chapter title is listed an optional theme, music or video. Some of readers may prefer to listen to this before, during, or after the reading of each chapter.

If before, you can play it soundlessly in your mind while reading. You enjoy reading as a kind of movie experience with music enhancing the experience. This feature is for you.

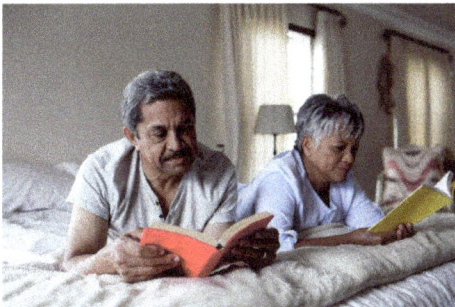

Other readers may find this a distraction. Or they may just want to avoid any online interference to their reading. These readers may have grown up in the early or even pre-television generations where radio stories dominated. That required imagination to supply the picture and any music. For them, we recommend skipping the optional themes entirely. This omission is for them.

The Discovery of Poison Ivy and Quicksand

Theme: *Poison Ivy* Coasters

"Two roads diverged in a wood and I—
I took the one less traveled by,
and that has made all the difference."

-Robert Frost

1940s
A Senior Pledge

The march of a thousand miles begins with a single step. And after that single step, we stop and rest.

Maybe a snack and a nap.

Diagnosis

Theme: *Pulling Back the Reins* K.D. Lang

As the decades since World War Two accumulate, many of the offbeat quotes of that time are forgotten. Here are a few I recall.

The entrance of America into the war changed everything. Hitler's army had inhabited France and was besieging England's last stand. And then the American troops flowed into Europe beginning with England, inhabiting a grateful nation.

Well, over time, there were some tensions. The American troops were at an age of great resources and larger appetites. This was one British response: *"The Yanks are over-fed, over-sexed, and OVER HERE!"*

Still, hospitality was abundant. As the war pushed back into Europe, thankful locals supplied home-brew alcohol to the soldiers as time allowed. This included a variety of Cognac with unique tasting alcohol, formula secret. So one medical unit slipped this Cognac into a batch of patient samples to be analyzed and diagnosed. The results were legendary. The diagnosis: ***"Your horse has kidney problems."***

Miss Kelly

Themes: *"Honeycomb"* Jimmie Rodgers; *"A Woman's Love"* Willie Nelson

Kindergarten is the official year of preschool in the American education system. Sure, outside earlier programs exist like Head Start in the United States and the historical Newstart in Canada.

Not to mention the far out (in?) earliest effort: the actual controversial Prenatal University founded in 1979 for brain stimulation of the late term fetus (graduation options for Caesarian or Breach students?).

But in the USA public school system, passing Kindergarten is the gateway to First Grade. First Grade! Number one! Like First Prize, top of the line! Then, after that, it's an annual descent into the less lofty numbers. Second Grade. Third. At the end of the next dozen years was Grade 12 (Grade 13 in Canada) and the high school diploma. But never as prestigious as that Grade #1.

Or so we told ourselves then. We needed to step up.

Children born in January or other winter months often had a problem starting kindergarten which began in September. They might begin early at age four or late a year older than the other children.

School officials usually stuck to the latter option, thereby delaying the whole educational process up to high school graduation.

Since I was already taller than the other children, my public school let me in at age four.

Still, it was a whole new experience for me.

I was surrounded by humans almost my size that seemed pretty bizarre. One girl ran circles around me saying *"I'm a bumble bee!"* and then buzzing. A boy needed a teacher's help to *"Go Potty"* since he had no idea how a toilet worked.

I was way too young to know what a movie stereotype of a back ward in a mental facility would be like, but my young imagination felt like I was there anyhow.

Where had my mother dropped me?

And then a giant came into my focus.

She said that she was my teacher, Miss Kelly.

And she welcomed me to the class.

I couldn't see her face though. She was standing and all I could see straight ahead were her legs.

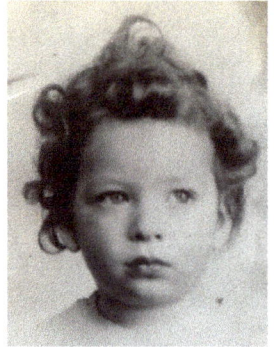

That friendly but commanding woman's beautiful voice seemed to come through the clouds.

Too soon for a four year old but I was in love.

Miss Kelly seated me in a chair by a very small desk. She asked what I liked to do when I play.

I said I liked to play chess or just walk around the city streets.

Neither of these choices seemed to engage her and she moved on.

President Roosevelt died that year. The ice man (no refrigerators then. just a wood ice box) asked me if I wanted to be the president someday. I said *"No! He died!"*

I spent that school year thinking about radio stories I had heard or books I had read or stories I made up for myself.

Often my imagination was interrupted by events which, if it came from Miss Kelly, my first love, had to be paid attention to.

My first report card, which I kept, had to be signed by a parent.

The written comment from Miss Kelly: *"Bobby is a very dreamy child and never feels the need to do a thing at once."*

World War Two had ended.

By my last report card, all the skills needed to begin first grade the following year were checked off.

I almost didn't make it because tying my own shoes was a problem to the last.

I hadn't been paying attention when how to do it was explained.

At the last minute, I invented a simpler way that I still do today, eight decades later.

I think Miss Kelly saw me do this my way but as long as my laces were tied securely, she checked it off as done.

Love validated.

The Buffalo Fruit Belt

Themes: *Sentimental Journey* Les Brown & Orchestra; *SOUND OF THE HOUND Radio Theme Big Heavy* George Lorenz/Cozy Eggleston 1957

1949. The first eight years of my life I was an only child.

At age eight, I did have both parents but my mother was recovering in the hospital and my father worked nights. Living on his income made us pretty poor. When I say poor: when we moved in our total furniture count was only two mattresses.

Being poor was fine with me. I loved to read or listen to the great radio shows. Each day had its wonders. The Black radio station had the best music too- rock and roll before there was rock and roll. It was hosted by *"The Hound"* (Theme *"Ah Woo! The Hounds Around!"*). The George Lorenz as the Hound inspired *Wolfman Jack* a generation later on the West Coast as in the movie *American Graffiti*.

No TV invented yet, internet, Zoom, and cell phones just a futuristic science fiction fantasy.

We lived in what has been considered to be the Harlem of Western New York State. It was where so many African-American families had just migrated to from the South seeking better safety and jobs. Streets were largely named for edible fruits: Lemon, Grape, and Peach. So there it was: the Fruit Belt. So-called even today.

I was in third grade at a school so desolate its name was a number: School Eight. The ancient building still had two entrances, one with a cemented label *"Girls"* overhead, the other of course labeled *"Boys"*. This apparent 19th century apartheid was ignored by us 20th century children. Hey, the World War had been over for four years now. New times. Our teachers were all white women while the students were majority Black. Civilizing us was clearly an agenda. Not as harsh as the Indian Boarding Schools. But a cultural-replacement was clearly the point. Boys had to arrive in white shirts and ties, girls in ankle length skirts. The mandatory gym exercise was a co-ed dancing instruction. The dancing? Square Dancing. In a brief nod to existing culture, our weekly whole grade-school assemblies began with a song- *"If I knew you were coming I'd a baked a cake ..."* And then we learned how lucky we were to be Americans. For an hour. Every Friday.

Across the street was an AME church with deep beautiful music and resonant chorus- including the loud passionate exclamations that somehow fit the music perfectly, enhancing everything else. When I was older I realized that all this was probably a funeral or other event of crushing sadness and the soulful music was from African roots as a way to cope. At that early age I just thought we were living in a magic place.

Of course the ministers of that church were a married couple that also owned most of the rentals their flock lived in, often several families to a tiny apartment. Hopeful and up from the South. Trusting their church. What ministers Mr. and Mrs. Brown didn't get from these renters, they got at their collection plate.

We did have landlords too though. An older Russian couple, the Ettengoffs, who lived below us. Even alone, if I walked across the floor in shoes, I would hear a banging from below. They were hitting their ceiling with a broom to let me know that I was making noise. I considered this. On special occasions like my birthday I would invite my whole grade school class to a party in our apartment. The pounding on our floor seemed rhythmic and was fine.

Saturdays were okay. I spent the afternoon in the movies. All was clear in the bathroom by the time I got home. Sundays were a different story. I had to get up earlier than my father or forget it. But one Sunday …

One Sunday morning, unread newspaper in hand, he left after an unusually brief visit. Plus he seemed happy, smiling. A rare light mood. Sure, he was finally rested, but something great was up.

He did go on to share the reason for his good mood: *"Your mother is coming back from the hospital today. When I bring her home, she will also have a baby brother for you."*

Wow. A baby brother?

I had actually asked for a pet monkey but a brother was a different okay. A gift was a gift.

Turned out, once he was home and I could see him, he was covered with thin black baby hair all over his body. I thanked my mother for the monkey but we both knew what he was. Further he was from the beginning put in my care. And in a few months his superfluous black fur was gone. Leaving behind a baby brother.

We all were pretty happy about that. I still am.

Then and Now.

1950s
Just Before Graduation in a 1950s High School

Theme: *Ain't that a Shame* Fats Domino

Yearbook lame signature additions:

2 Good

+2 Be

=4 Gotten

Or

You don't know me but I'm signing anyhow.

Rebel without Sausages

Substitute Teacher Writing on Board

"Punctuate this sentence":

Fun Fun Fun Worry Worry Worry Silence. No Takers. Substitute Teacher waits a few seconds.

Then she answers her own question:

"Okay. Fun period, Fun period, Fun NO period, Worry! Worry! Worry!"

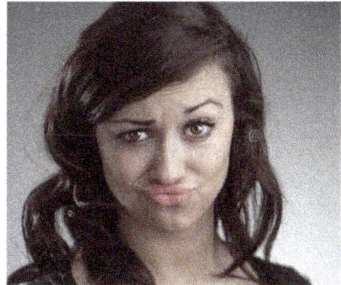

Cold Tale

Theme: *Wake up Old Lady* Lightning Hopkins

Two deviled egg chicks on a plate in the fridge. One says to the other: *"Where's our mother?"*

The other says: *"Not no mystery... She's that rotisserie"*.

Buffalo Postal

Theme: *Ote'a Tekou - Mahealani* Uchiyama

At 99 my father's father liked to proclaim that he had come to Buffalo as a young man for its climate. Buffalo? Land of the continual 10 foot snow drifts black with pollution? He went on that Buffalo had no war, famine, earthquakes, volcanoes, tsunamis, or typhoons. My grandfather found happiness in appreciating the missing negatives. Dodging the bullet was more than enough for his good life.

Typhoons were in fact hurricanes from the largest ocean, the so-called Pacific. Not so pacified in a typhoon where the immense expanse of water could generate 200 mph winds and the typical horizontal rain. Buffalo had only the Great Lakes though that was enough for the year's ten months of snow and two months of hot humidity.

Holiday Storm

In the winter of 1957, my father got me hired as a temporary postal worker for the Christmas rush. He was a supervisor and much respected, even more from the people of color who he treated fairly. I was 16.

My first job was to pack letters and packages in a mail bag to hand off to the railway mail for transport. I filled it up to the top, heavy, and dragged it to the waiting train. Two large men jumped off and tried to lift it to their rail car.

"Hey kid! This is too full! Too heavy! You're just supposed to fill it halfway!"

One of them stood by the bag while the other went to complain to the supervisor. My father came back with the railway worker. Listened to them complain about how I had made the bag too heavy to lift. He nodded, lifted the bag with one hand and tossed it into the rail car. Said *"They can't handle a bag more than half full. They're fragile!"*

The rail workers retreated with no more comment, shutting the rail car entrance from within.

My father was no larger than they were and had a herniated painful back. Not supposed to lift anything heavy. I apologized for packing the bag too high and right off the bat causing him a problem.

He smiled, said the day was still young, plenty of time for more trouble. He seemed happy, even with me. Who *was* this man? I sure liked this work version.

My next post was a room full of letters to sort into their delivery holes. Just me to do it. A chance to show I could do hard work and fast. In an hour I had the whole room sorted, no mail left unfiled. Just in time for two postal workers from the next shift to get there.

"Hey kid! You didn't leave anything for us to sort! Trying to get us fired?"

This complaint soon got to my father and made him laugh when we were alone. He was glad I had discovered the expected government tempo.

I spent the rest of my first full day tossing Christmas packages on a conveyer belt.

My partner there, like a lot of postal workers, was retired military looking for some extra holiday cash. He was bitter, tired, and grumpy. Maybe wanted to test me as well.

Saying *"Watch this!"* he set aside a decorated box marked "*FRAGILE. TOYS*". Putting it at the very beginning of the slow moving conveyer belt, he selected a parcel marked "*HEAVY. FARM MACHINERY*" and dropped it on top of the box of toys. Laughed.

He next found a box that smelled of something sweet, ripped it open to find some little girl's expensive doll. He leaned over, spit a big glob on its forehead, and resealed the package.

This man was easily more than 40 years older than me. Was he trying to make me laugh? Thought all this was funny? I wasn't laughing.

I pointed up to the ceiling where the postal inspectors had their observation holes from the floor above.

He just said *"Forget it! There's nobody there. Anyway, they just get hired to keep us from stealing the mail. They don't give a damn what we do to it on the way. This is CHRISTMAS and THIS is what I think of it!"* He stockpiled more farm machinery for his next fragile targets.

I said I didn't want any part of whatever he was working through. Seemed to me by then that his testing me was leading to some mail theft. I took a bathroom break.

The postal inspectors got a tip to keep an eye on him, never mind who tipped them. By the end of the day he was led away in handcuffs. A holiday he'll remember.

Summer 1958: The Calm in the Storm

Now 17, this was my summer between high school and college. I got a job for a month as a temp again in the Buffalo post office. To the dismay of my parents, I loved being there.

The work was hard and so built muscle. No homework- when the shift was over it was done. The people were interesting, funny, mostly friendly. I learned to swear in many languages, especially Polish, Italian, German, Gaelic, Spanish, Canadian French.

In the Fall, I would use the New York State Regents scholarship I'd won in a statewide exam to go to college. Though it had to be in New York State. Dreams of California and Hawaii deferred.

But for that Summer, lasting endlessly at my age then, I was a postal worker.

My father regretted never going to college, feeling at first that being a working man was as noble as you could get. He sure didn't want me to take his path. My mother, a teacher, was even stronger on this point.

Which is why they never approved of the lifelong friend I made at that post office: Tom Crowley. I argued that, besides being a creative photographer, he was a decent hardworking young friend who was doing his best to support his wife and the medical bills for their blue baby boy.

Blue? Heart not working right. Life threatening.

Not much later there was his funeral with so much grief that a parental divorce followed.

Yet for the rest of his long life, Tom became the older brother I had been missing.

We went in together to buy a very unusual car for $50: the Isetta. It had a motorcycle engine and a front that was also the door. Overhead was a removable roof.

Tom had the license so we were set. Explored *"Buffalo after Dark"* throughout the summer.

Tom at my age had joined the Coast Guard. Said the music was always country. We sang some of these classics as we drove- *There Stands a Glass* and *It Don't Hurt Any More.* Lucky nobody else heard us as our Isetta made its way through the fruit belt ghetto at night. Except at stop lights.

I do recall one of Tom's Coast Guard stories. One of the ship's officers made harassing Tom a priority. He was constantly sending the teenage Tom to clean the latrine for any real or imagined sin. Followed by white glove inspections. Leading to more latrine duty. Such a white glove inspection was scheduled one day, this time including the Captain and the Ship Surgeon. Tom knew that his officer nemesis was trying to get him thrown out of the coast guard. He prepared by smuggling a small blob of peanut butter into the latrine. With just minutes before the inspection began, he went to the last toilet in the row, swabbed the seat with alcohol disinfectant, and then placed the peanut butter ball on one side of the seat. The inspection began as always with Tom's nemesis leading the charge. The Captain looked annoyed with these antics but reluctantly followed. The ship's surgeon just looked bored. Until the hostile officer waved them in to see the last toilet seat in the row. Pointing to the peanut butter ball on the seat, he bellowed *"Crowley! What's THAT?"* Tom just got out a *"Sorry!"* before grabbing the ball and swallowing it.

He did spend a few days in Sick Bay but recovered quickly, better yet knowing his nemesis had been ejected from the ship by a concerned Captain and a no longer bored surgeon.

No wonder Tom's goodbye all those years was *"Squeeze it easy"*.

Then the Monsoon

Toward the end of the Summer, I met a celebrity at the post office, Gino Marella.

He was a young college wrestler from Rochester, near Buffalo, and had been undefeated at every match as of that date. These were real contests, unscripted. He was said, accurately, to be on his way to greatness.

My father brought him over to meet me, smiling all the way.

To this day I don't recall if he was just visiting or a temp. This was the only time I ever saw him. I was seeing somebody taller than me and probably hundreds of pounds of muscle heavier.

He was eventually 6 feet 6" 440 pounds.

GORILLA MONSOON

But that day he was smiling too, Held out a massive hand to shake.

I took the hand and was surprised. He was shaking my hand with just two fingers and a thumb, *very* gently. We talked for a few minutes before my father moved him along to meet more people.

Now I was already over six feet tall myself and hadn't expected the light handshake from this budding athlete. So I asked my father why such a colossus had given me that dainty shake. My father explained *"He just didn't want to break the bones in your hand."*

As the years went on, Gino remained undefeated in genuine matches. But then joined the wrestling we know today. Gino sang in Italian before his matches. Next he became *"Gorilla Monsoon"* and, even so, retained a reputation as the best living wrestler of his time.

About to move into his forties, he staged a fight with Muhammed Ali in which neither was hurt. Although Ali clearly was a great and tolerant sport.

Muhammed Ali vs Gorilla Monsoon
June 2, 1976 at Philadelphia Arena

The Monsoon ran the franchise for a while, became a commentator, and was the celebrated wrestler of all time he had been expected to be.

I'll bet he never had to sort mail or packages.

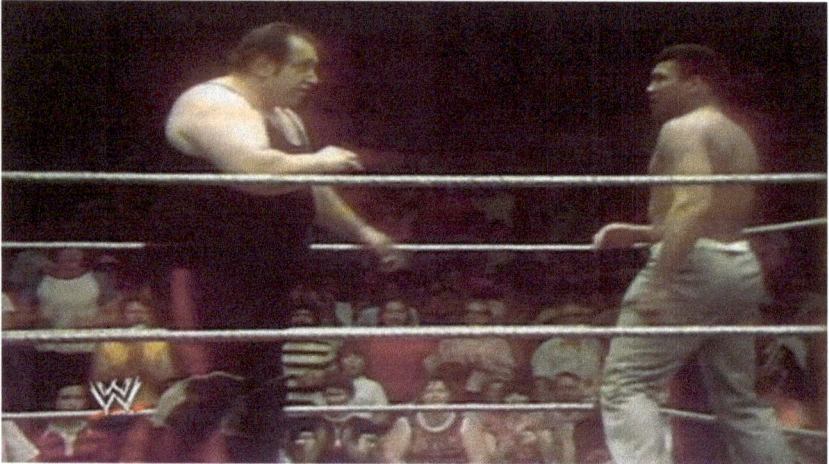

©2012 boxinghalloffame.com
Luxor Hotel Las Vegas

The Bride's Sandwich

"Luck is what happens when preparation meets opportunity"
Seneca

Summer was coming to a close and so was my postal job.

Good friends, good pay, great exercise. No desire for this as a career.

No regrets either. Seeing my father so revered as he was at work was well worth the time in itself. Taught me a lot about how supervision should be.

And about blue collar humor.

The new guy was friendly enough but his constant good cheer was more happiness than somebody we worked with could handle.

The groom's fine mood was undoubtedly reflecting his new bride's love.

Which manifested each lunch time in a steak sandwich for her husband, one with all the trimmings, encased in a brand new lunch bag. One inscribed with his name on it. Sitting in the communal refrigerator. Unmolested that first day, eaten happily by her husband.

Another bagged and inscribed steak sandwich was refrigerated day two by her husband. But at lunchtime it was missing. Stolen!

On day three, we all kept an eye open for our new friend's sandwich. But no, the bag had disappeared again by lunchtime.

The bride was not having this. She again prepared her now famous steak sandwich for her loved one. Laced in a fresh new bag with his name boldly written upon it. On day four, it was placed I the refrigerator as always.

Almost. She had supplemented the steak spread with a generous helping of horse laxative.

The sandwich disappeared before lunch break.

Not long after, one of the postal workers bent over with a groan and collapsed.

Those carrying him out to the ambulance held their breath against the fecal stench.

The bride's sandwiches continued unmolested thereafter.

Post sandwich: Jokes about horse laxative and horses in general abounded in my last week on this job.

Most memorable for me was a regular who had been given three double shifts in a row by an unpleasant manager. Nor was the air conditioning working on this very hot and humid day.

During a visit by the region's administrator on his third and last double shift, the exhausted postal worker emerged from his sweaty task minus any clothing below the waist.

When questioned by the administrator, he replied:

> *"If I have to work like a horse, I'm going to look like a horse."*

Buffalo Goodbyes

Themes: *Fingertips* Stevie Wonder

From my time in the post office in the 1950s I had learned multi-lingual insults in Polish, German, Italian, Gaelic, and a variety of other cultures, especially African-American.

Yet I hadn't realized how my own daily language had been influenced.

Until years later when I had children of my own as the only parent for young daughters.

When I spoke from that time when I had been their age in Buffalo, I was now gifted with many useful corrections. My daughter Cinnamon was fearless but brief in gently correcting my questionable Buffalonian language.

Her sister Angel, my youngest, was equally fearless, relentless too. She had a message to deliver and deliver it she would. I teased back. We usually ended laughing.

A sample: *"Dad. Please turn off that Dan Hicks record 'How can I miss you when you won't go away?' Thanks, very Buffalo. Now. When people say goodbye or something friendly like 'HAVE A NICE DAY', you should not respond with the usual 'SAME TO YOU! Try something else."*

"No! 'MAY YOU GET EVERYTHING YOU DESERVE!' is worse."

"How about a goodbye from your kind fatherly point of view?"

"Umm, 'SQUEEZE IT EASY!' is not that."

"Let's try this. You are walking and a friend sees you, comes over for a minute of conversation, then leaves saying 'SEE YA!' How do you say goodbye to him?"

"'NOT IF I SEE YOU FIRST'? How are you ever going to get along with our friends if you say goodbye to them in that Buffalo way?"

"Okay. Any GOOD advice on what you can say when you say goodbye to our friends? 'LIVE WITH IT'? Really?"

"Oh! I was doing my best not to laugh. Just came out."

"Fine, I'll 'live with it'. Thanks Dad. Great advice!"

End Theme: *Isn't She Lovely* Stevie Wonder

Three Thanksgiving Dinners

Theme: *Reunion* Bobbie Gentry

1950

My father worked the "graveyard shift" which meant all night long. He got home by 7:30 AM, ate anything he could quickly find in the kitchen, and then slept through the day. By 5:00 PM he was done with this hibernation and soon at the table with a bear's appetite. In a few hours he would be leaving for another night's work again. Even on Thanksgiving, he would leave on time as the graveyard shift was considered the next day.

My brother was 18 months old and almost done with baby food. This Thanksgiving it would still be Gerbers. I was 9 years old and a voracious reader in these pre-TV/computer days. Thanks to that I knew Gerbers had been caught selling baby food replete with insect parts and rat droppings. Many times. Each of these episodes led to a corporate fine all of $100. I objected to my brother being fed Gerbers but so far without success. This Thanksgiving he would dine on that baby food again, seasoned with rodent and mixed bugs to taste. Chewy no doubt.

My mother had been a high school Microbiology teacher and would be so again in another year. In the meantime she shopped for this holiday with meager funds. We lived on my father's minimum wage income alone, qualifying as almost poor enough to be homeless, just barely able to rent a place in the saddest part of town. During the war she had waited once a week in line for hours at a butcher shop with her ration coupon in hand. Now the war had been over for five years, she still went to the same butcher. He always kept some inexpensive *"gourmet meats"* for her, cuts that people were *"too ignorant"* to want. These included organ meats, tails and ears (maybe even eyes?), and, on special occasions: cow's tongue. Bovine livers you could bread and smother with onions (didn't work for me) while the body parts could be machined into ground beef. This Thanksgiving my parents and I each were looking at a plate holding only one large piece of meat. The unadorned cow's tongue.

I actually tried a bite. It was in all ways still a tongue. As an adult I might have said *"I don't French kiss cows"* or something equally lame but, no worries, as an adult Bossie's huge tongue and I would never again meet. At nine though, despite hunger, I spit out the bite and ran for the bathroom. My mother yelled *"Are you sick?"* Nope, I was just fast returning with my toothbrush and toothpaste. They were not amused. My father, having wolfed down his own cow tongue, reached for mine.

This precipitated an argument. My mother pointed out that I was already way too thin, nearly six feet tall and only 145 pounds. My father reasonably argued that if I didn't want it, well, he always ate whatever we didn't. A garbage disposal would have been wasted on us.

To the surprise of both of them, I blessed his choice.

Without further debate my former bovine tongue disappeared past his.

Going to bed hungry that night I wasn't dreaming of a roast turkey with stuffing.

Instead, being realistic for the times, I longed for a cheeseburger. This was years before McDonalds served its first 15 cent hamburger, a culinary revelation fitting my college student budget at the time.

More recently I learned from a friend at Burger King that they grind their own beef on site for the hamburgers. Grinding is from bovine parts buyers shun in their original form. They grind up organ meats including the liver, ears, the end that goes over the fence last, and, yes, tongues. So maybe I still had the tongue in hamburger form a few times.

Just not in a shape to need a toothbrush after.

The next year my mother returned to her job, doubling the family income. No time for her to cook much anymore.

So my life was saved by TV dinners, chip steaks, grilled cheese and tomato soup, and anything else I could quickly cook. Nor would I ever feed my brother *Gerbers*. With the better family income, he was raised in a less "food insecure" home.

Still, the image of that Thanksgiving tongue on my plate stays with me.

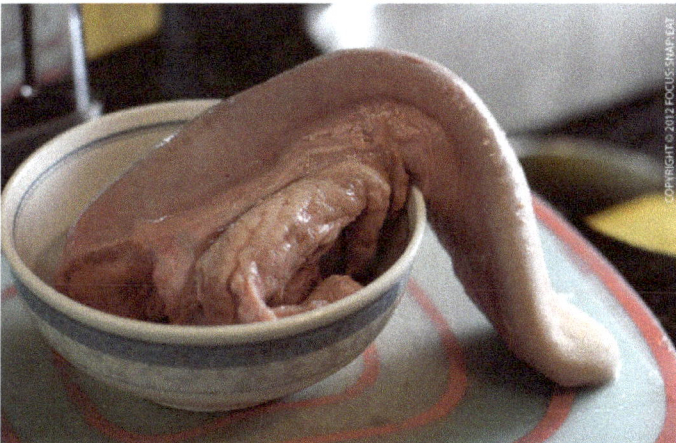

1985

My mother was one of fourteen children. Five of her nine brothers became medical doctors.

One, Sidney, was, with help from Ted Williams, a founder of Boston's Dana Farber Clinic. There his patients were children fighting Leukemia, a death sentence in those days. Every night he tucked each one of his child guests into bed, doing all he could think of to have them survive another day. He invented the first drug treatment for this, becoming the "Father of Chemotherapy". Another brother, Harold, became the President of his own insurance company. The eldest son, Marvin, became a philosophy professor, bringing the European phenomenologists to our country just in time to avoid being gassed to death by the Nazis.

My favorite, Dan, was an adventurer, successful at enjoying life fully.

How did Simon Farber, the immigrant stevedore father of these 14 children get so many sons through school? He worked multiple jobs as long as he could and, as can happen in a large family, the older children helped the younger ones. This included my mother who always sent home as much of her salary as possible until she married at 30, an advanced age for the day.

What career paths were there then for her and her four sisters? Or any women living a century ago. My mother, Evelyn, wanted very much to be a doctor too. But she had been born in 1908 and women in her day had but only a few careers other than "house-wife". These alternatives usually were nursing or teaching. Evelyn got her teaching credential and continued through graduate work in Microbiology.

But her family needed her help so she began decades of work as a teacher. At this she was successful, even teaching a high school Microbiology class. She was so loved by her students that, for several years in a row, their Yearbook was dedicated to her. Then she retired.

Microbiology was as close as she ever formally got to being a medical doctor. Still, retired, she now had time at home to increase her informal medical practice without a license. Her husband and two sons were the hostage patients.

Other than that, her new post-retirement career mission was to be a great cook. Food soon integrated into her realm of home medical practice, allowing what she considered to be healthy or restorative components to every meal. Sadly, by her age she had been deprived of substantial taste bud competence. Her food then tasted awful.

Who knew what she had added into any given meal? She was a great fan of laxatives for one thing.

My father still needed sustenance. He too came from a large family of nine children. He ate fast. He ate anything. He ate whatever we did not. This made him her star patient when it came to her culinary practice.

Not so for my brother, which may still have helped him survive the food insecure streets during his Haight-Ashbury years.

As for me, I had continued as a skeletal teenager, surviving on TV dinners and meals at the homes of friends. I also used every opportunity to make my own meals from whatever was available. Complete feasts that way would continue to be tomato soup and grilled cheese, a thinly sliced chip steak on a slice of toast, or the World War II specialty understood as "Shit on a Shingle" (ham and peas on a slice of toast).

When we ran out of hot dogs, I learned that a hot dog roll filled with relish, onion, coleslaw, mustard, and ketchup tasted just fine without the hot dog.

Summer trips to Canada taught me that fries go fine with vinegar (try it) if you have no ketchup. The beverage of choice was tap water or Vernors Ginger Ale. In later years I learned to make a few special dishes like leg of lamb slow cooked with green maraschino cherries or fried bananas with lemon sauce. Or omelets purple with grape juice.

When cooking for my two daughters though, they preferred to each do their own cooking. Maybe it was the green food coloring I added to scrambled eggs or most other things I served. I did green eggs and ham before Dr. Seuss made it known.

My mother *was* good at making desserts. They were delicious and a staple. So our nutrition was impaired as well.

Years later I was invited to a home office party in San Francisco. My charge was to bring "green food". I brought green ice cream and green treats from the "Citizen Cake" store. Childhood strikes deep.

The grandchildren felt much the same as my brother and I about their grandmother's cooking.

On holidays we would all gather at the home of my parents. Grandchildren waited until Grandma Evelyn had stepped out of the room to dump their plates of food in the fireplace, covering it with ashes.

Eventually, at one Thanksgiving family gathering in 1985, years into this clean plate technique, my father started a long overdue cleaning of the fireplace.

As he worked through the years of holiday meals past, he was good natured about it all.

Finally finished, he stood and announced to us: *"That was like an archeological dig!"*

2020

The year of the pandemic, climate change floods, fires, typhoons, hurricanes, and tornadoes, lethal racist hatred, and presiding over all this: Donald Trump.

From all of this, unemployment and sudden poverty matched the Great Depression from a century before. By Thanksgiving, donated food lines for the "food insecure" (starving) also matched those in the Great Depression, going on for miles, but this time mostly in cars.

San Francisco's hotel row was over years plagued by flocks of pigeons, especially from all the white excretions everywhere. Somehow there aren't as many to be found there anymore. As the homeless population grew, and now the food insecure joining them, pigeon survival plummeted.

(Once in Thailand I visited their version of a KFC and ordered two drumsticks, only to be served two tiny versions that definitely appeared to have originated on a pigeon. So, an international wave going on?)

Our Thanksgiving this year was family only by phone, other families by Zoom. Nearly half of the nation was facing homelessness. Half a million Americans had already died in the continuing pandemic. Climate change was accelerating.

We were thankful that we were among those that still survived, roof over our heads. Post-election hope was growing, vaccines for the pandemic were on the horizon, the youth were overall much more aware than prior generations and even more willing to struggle for a better future.

Many of us somehow ate turkey or chicken with trimmings that day.

We will hold our breath as best we can for the New Years to come.

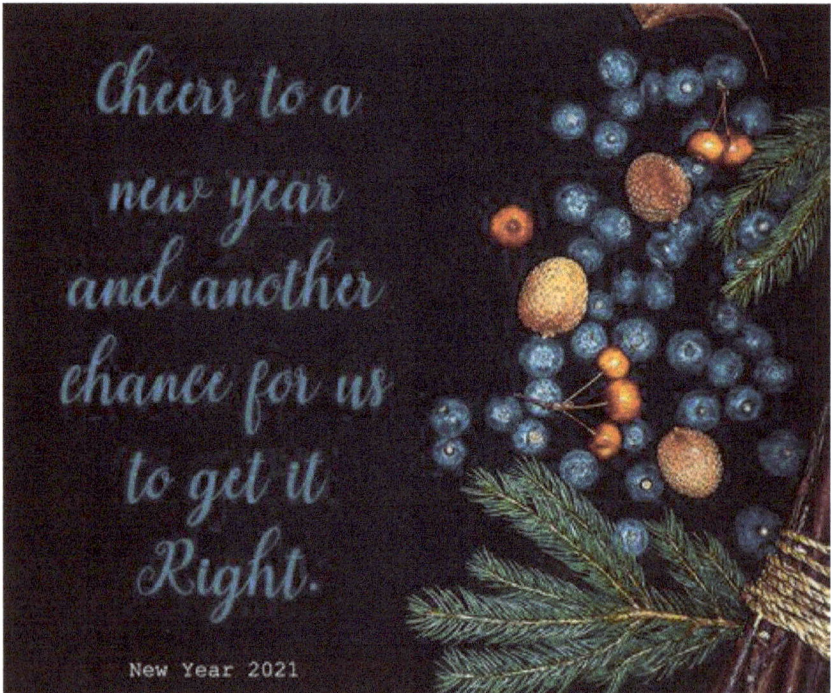

Cheers to a new year and another chance for us to get it Right.

New Year 2021

Madstop

Theme: *Great Grandfather* Bo Diddley

Clarkson 60+ Years Ago

My first two years of college (1958-1960) were as a Physics major in an engineering college.

Clarkson College, now Clarkson University, was in North America's coldest spot at the top of upstate New York (yes, I lived in Alaska and Clarkson's town, Potsdam, was colder). The temperature was usually about 20 degrees below zero during the day, rising to 40 degrees below zero at night.

"Madstop" was how we pronounced it (Potsdam backwards).

Clarkson College's motto was *"The workman that needeth not to be ashamed"*. Though often our mentors could have used a little shame. My mechanical drawing prof was a fine example.

Grades as Personality

Professor Myron Mochel taught using free hand diagrams designed to create products for those who chose to build them, often by his own demonstration. I'm not an artist and this was validated often as I did my best to recreate his personal masterpieces. Ones so complex most of us never really did them justice when we tried to reproduce them.

This probably didn't help. One day he dared us to bring any two dimensional drawing into class. He would then show us how effectively and rapidly he'll put it on the blackboard, exactly scaled and detailed such that anybody could build it.

When he said he was ready to pick a student's contribution, I deliberately yawned and looked out the window. So of course he took my drawing first, an object that was an illusion much like Escher's. After many heroic but futile attempts to schematically draw the illusion so that it could be built, he finally realized that it could not exist in real space. The class laughed loud and long.

Mochler though overlooked the comedic aspects completely. So I was not his favorite.

More telling as to his character was his grading scheme. His measurement of our work products, and ultimate grade, was on this scale: A, B, C, D, F, 2F, 3F, 4F, and 5F. This since, clearly, a single F could not accurately or fully express his overwhelming disdain for our work. The grade of 5F counted five times an F for a single work product grade and, by sure and certain design, devastatingly impacted each overall class grade.

In this measurement constellation, an average student's final grade would be "F". Maybe some pride in that as a grade from the middle of the range? By the end of the class I anticipated such an average grade at best. And yet, he passed me!

Pushing my luck, a common action, I asked him how I could have earned a passing (above the average F) grade in his class, given his measurement system. He scowled and said he just didn't want me to take his class again.

The Generational Secret of Clarkson College

It was the spring of 1959 in Potsdam. The snow was almost gone.

The school semester still had some months to go until the end of my first year in this remote engineering college.

Classes began six mornings a week. Dodging man-size Damocles style icicles on the way to class was the usual gauntlet. Hard to breathe in this alien world of low temperatures, found each day throughout the nine months of school. The slippery ice along the way for those morning trips was soon countered by shoes with massive treads at bottom, ones insensitively but literally called *"Guinea Ground Grabbers"*.

Why was I here?

I had been one of a few high school seniors that had won a New York State scholarship through high scores on a competitive written exam. There was a catch. It had to be a college in New York State.

Gone were my dreams of going to a university in the brand new state of Hawaii. Climate paradise for anybody growing up in Buffalo. My parents thought of the University of Hawaii as only teaching basket weaving and hula dancing. I had done research and knew better. My Hawaii plan had no backers though (later to be reimagined by public awareness from the TV show *Hawaii 5-0*).

Now the scholarship bound me to New York. So where there?

At 17 my career plans were more or less to actualize the best of science fiction. Learn the true nature of the cosmos. For this I chose to be a Physics Major.

By chance I met a graduate of Clarkson College. He said he had loved it there. And it was a great place to study the mysteries of Physics.

Never mind the cold climate and the all-male student population (shaving and bathing in the absence of females was sporadic). He thought that if I had survived 17 years in Buffalo weather, I could survive anywhere.

Finally, he shared the generational Clarkson secret: *"Don't tell them unless they can't figure it out for themselves"* he said. *"Give them some time"* he said. So I was sworn to temporary secrecy. And went to Clarkson. Well, the state was paying for it, most of it, so I gave it a try. Took me awhile to realize that no cosmology or actualized fiction would be taught there. Instead it seemed to be training us as electricians and plumbers. Yes: *"Workmen that needed not to be ashamed"*.

Also, not yet having mastered mathematics, or even having been casually introduced, I was in a strange country without knowing the required language. My only high grades were in "Liberal Studies" classes consisting of everything not Engineering or Physics. A message there.

Earaches

I did enjoy doing a weekly satirical radio show on WNTC called ***"Earaches"***. My opening theme was Bo Diddley's *"Great Grandfather"*, followed by me saying in as deep a voice as I could muster at 17: *"My name is Morgan. Yours I don't need."* Between early rock & roll music breaks were my Stan Freberg style satire pieces and taped interviews, usually done in the spacious but busy dormitory restroom for the echo effect, barring flushes.

The satire pieces got me kicked off the air a few times. I had fun with our funding sponsor, Winston Cigarettes. Each time that happened I talked myself into being back on the air. So my listener base grew, eventually reaching near 100% of the students for that hour.

My favorite interview was with the Mayor of Potsdam who was being charged with gross embezzlement by a grand jury. He argued that as Mayor he was responsible for a million dollar operation, so that fact alone should mean he had better not be distracted by such charges. There was still a lot of money left. He refused to resign. As I recall, he finished his term still not in jail.

I was having fun in this little carrier current radio station, rooms sound insulated with empty egg cartons on the walls.

The show eventually lasted the two years I was at Clarkson. Although in the winter of year two I moved from all Rock & Roll breaks to playing Hawaiian Music while urging every listener to move to that warmer climate. Vic Dawley, in the class a year behind me, continued this good work after I left.

Future Roomies

I would leave after my second year at Clarkson, to transfer to Michigan State University (MSU) and a better choice of major then in Psychology. Ironically, it was there that I finally learned math and how to use it. Too late for Clarkson. At MSU, even though I was a junior there, all students in their first year, transfer or not, were required to spend that year in a dormitory. I was assigned to live in the one for administration-defined misfits: meaning foreign students, returning vets, transfers, discipline problems, writers. A truly creative mix.

Here I will just include a nod to my own roommates in that dorm, Bryan Hall.

The first was Gilbert Moore, a poet from Montreal. He realized by the close of the first term there that his poetic future was somewhat ignored in Michigan. He raced to be back home in Montreal.

Without a roommate, I began the second term gifted with a late entering freshman roommate, a local and very young Alan "Mike" Mikesell. Mike's father promised that if his grades for that beginning term were all "As" he would be gifted with a car. A gift for the rest of us on our dorm floor too we realized. We needed a sure thing. I had Mike enroll in the least challenging Football Players courses: Golf, Exercise, and "Ice Cream". The last class provided complete information on the history, manufacture, sales, and variety of the dessert. Mike got his As. But not the car. His father was not impressed with Mike's courses. Golf? Ice Cream? Mike got sent home, hopefully to try again eventually.

My third and last MSU roommate was Arthur David Otterbridge Hodgson. He was without a roommate too and we consolidated by moving into the same room before MSU could choose for us. Arthur had no roommate because he was black and his original roommate had been white. That roomie's mother would have none of that and yanked her son out of the dorm. Arthur was a soccer player and head of the Campus United Nations. From Bermuda, it was his ambition to go back there when he graduated and lead his country to independence from England. Looking like a young athletic Malcom X, I believed him. He had two strategies for this:

1. Sign up to give a speech at the real United Nations in New York. Any citizen of a member country can do this but the wait is years. For Arthur, he had it timed for graduation.

2. Apply for a Rhodes graduate award in his major of Economics. This would involve an apprenticeship with the head of state of a developing country followed by a more settled democracy in Europe.

As to the first, his timing was on target. As a member of his minority political party in Bermuda, their party leaders, faced with the reality of his speaking for them at the UN, appointed him forthwith as their representative on the (British) Governor's Council. Despite this prestigious and very visible role, he drove a cab during the day, dressing down in Tee shirt and jeans. He wore the same clothes to the governing Council, which delighted the younger generation. Moreso when he dressed up in suit and tie for his sister's wedding to make his values clear. Arthur was a fine orator and gave a great speech advocating freedom from colonial status. As to the second, his Rhodes fellowship came through. He would wind it up studying economics in Scandinavia. First though he would be off to study with Fidel Castro, the new head of an independent Cuba. Castro was too busy it turned out, shunting Arthur off to Cuba's Finance Minister, Che Guevera. Arthur eventually went back to Bermuda and did his best to achieve independence. That hasn't happened yet, even in this century despite his best efforts. Bermuda remains the oldest British colony with Queen Elizabeth the head of state. Arthur today is a retired judge in his home country. Bermuda has great beaches.

Before all of this though we both had one more year, outside the dorm at last, to graduate. Having become friends we rented a place together.

Back to Clarkson in late 1958

Still, when 1959 was getting closer, I wondered: should I announce the secret?

First this: When I had left for Clarkson in the Fall of 1958, I was a tall skeletal teenager weighing 145 pounds. The food at the college was terrible but the cold weather and unrelenting pace made us ravenous for it. Sure we found pennies and hair in the food. The "mystery meat" remained a mystery. The cook's dog helped lick the used plates clean for her. Despite all this I arrived home for Thanksgiving heavier by forty pounds of muscle now weighing in at 185. My mother couldn't believe it. Or didn't want to. Let's explore this for a minute.

Food in the Fireplace

My mother was one of fourteen children. Five of her nine brothers became medical doctors. Sidney, with help from Ted Williams, was a founder of Boston's Dana Farber Clinic. There his patients were children fighting Leukemia, a death sentence in those days. Every night he tucked each one of his child guests into bed, doing all he could think of to have them survive another day. He invented the first drug treatment for this, becoming the "Father of Chemotherapy". Another brother, Harold, became the President of his own insurance company. The eldest son, Marvin, became a philosophy professor, bringing the European phenomenologists to our country just in time to avoid being gassed to death by the Nazis. My favorite, Dan, was an adventurer, successful at enjoying life fully.

How did Simon Farber, the immigrant stevedore father of these 14 children get so many sons through school? He worked multiple jobs as long as he could and, as can happen in a large family, the older children helped the younger ones. This included my mother who always sent home as much of her salary as she could until she married at the advanced age for the day of 30. What career paths for her and her four sisters? Or any women living a century ago.

My mother, Evelyn, wanted very much to be a doctor too. Her family needed her help so she began decades of work as a teacher. At this she was successful, even teaching a high school Microbiology class. She was so loved by her students that, for several years in a row, their Yearbook was dedicated to her. Then she retired.

Microbiology was as close as she ever formally got to being a medical doctor. Still, retired, she now had time at home to increase her informal medical practice without a license. Her husband and two sons were the hostage patients.

Other than that, her new post-retirement self-chosen career mission was to be a great cook. Food soon integrated into her realm of home medical practice, allowing what she considered to be healthy or restorative components to every meal. Sadly, by her age she had been deprived of substantial taste bud competence. Her food then tasted awful. Who knew what she had added to any given meal? She was a great fan of laxatives for one thing.

My father worked hard and needed sustenance. He too came from a large family of nine children. He ate fast. He ate anything. He ate whatever we did not. This made him her star patient when it came to the culinary practice. Not so for my brother, which may have helped him survive on the streets during his Haight-Ashbury years. As for me, I continued as a skeletal teenager, surviving on TV dinners and meals at the homes of friends. I also used every opportunity to make my own meals from whatever was available. Complete feasts that way would be tomato soup and grilled cheese, a thinly sliced chip steak on a slice of toast, or the World War II specialty understood as *"Shit on a Shingle"* (ham and peas on a slice of toast). When we ran out of hot dogs, I learned that a hot dog roll filled with relish, onion, coleslaw, mustard, and ketchup tasted just fine without the dog. Summer trips to Canada taught me that fries go fine with vinegar (try it) if you have no ketchup. The beverage of choice was tap water or Vernors Ginger Ale. In later years I learned to make a few special dishes like leg of lamb slow cooked with green maraschino cherries or fried bananas with lemon sauce. Or omelets purple with grape juice. When cooking for my two daughters though, they preferred to each do their own cooking. Maybe it was the green food coloring I added to scrambled eggs or most other things I served. I did green eggs and ham before Dr. Seuss made it known.

My mother was good at making deserts though. They were delicious and a staple. So our nutrition was impaired as well. Years later I was invited to a home office party in San Francisco. My charge was to bring "green food". I brought green ice cream and green treats from the "Citizen Cake" store. Childhood strikes deep.

Back in the 1950s, Clarkson food was a step up. Not a great step. But up. Maybe photos might help. These are on the next page.

The photo record

<u>Photo A</u>. A typical dormitory shot. Hygiene was sparse in all male dorms.

An earlier roommate of mine was from Japan. Hirofumi Matsusaki. Japanese are tightly packed on an island country. They tolerate this by daily bathing and devoted cleanliness. Not so in our dormitory.

For me, growing up poor, the once-a-week bath was on Saturday night; so-called sponge baths with a wet washcloth were done other days.

Hirofumi and I definitely influenced each other. For me, though it didn't take until a year or two later, I eventually arrived at a devoted daily bathing regime. Dating maybe had something to do with this. But no women to impress, or not repulse, in the Clarkson dorm.

Hirofumi for his part did not return after the first Thanksgiving break. Looking him up on the internet in this more current century, I found him to be celebrated in Japan as an inventive chemical engineer successful with fragrance products.

Maybe I had a little something to do with that career choice.

A

B

C

D

E

F

My substitute roommate that first year was George Zabriskie or "Zips". He was a great fan of Chet Atkins who I heard nonstop in our room for the rest of the year. Zips plastered the bulletin board over his dorm bed with Playboy Playmate pictures. We had a desk in the middle of the small dorm room, between the separate beds, so when we studied we faced each other from our respective sides. This gave me a scenic view of his Playmate photos.

To fill my own Bulletin Board, I posted a large very colorful chart my mother had sent me called "the infant stool cycle". Zips found this hard to view, despite the Chet Atkins perpetual soundtrack. Periodically he would lean back and throw himself at an angle so he could look at his own Bulletin Board.

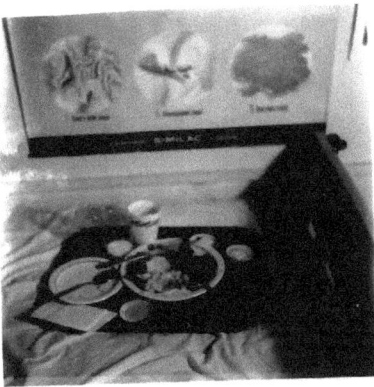

Zips became a good friend. I missed him when he didn't return for the second Clarkson year. About 40% of the rest of our class weren't back then either.

That second year, I had the best Clarkson dorm roommate: Douglas Griffin, seen in Photo A sitting and holding his nose while our neighbor from the next room shared armpit fragrance in his typical gesture of sharing.

I'm still in touch with Doug, even though I was one of those not returning in year three. Doug went the full distance, got his degree, and did a career with IBM.

I found a hole in the middle of my dorm mattress but, rebuffed for a better one, got used to it. I joked with Doug that the hole was for easing my sexual tensions though it was far too small. When his father came to visit, he asked to see my famous mattress hole. Left me impressed by the great relationship he had with his Dad.

Most in the dorm were learning to be engineers. Different subspecialties could be competitive. For example, I announced on my show the rumor that the urinals were all about to be raised a few inches so as to keep the double EEs (electrical engineers) on their toes. Apparently they were deemed to be shorter.

The dorm had many characters, too many to expand on here. The largest among us, for example, was Karl Trout who naturally was nicknamed "Guppy". Required to post our own shortened nickname on our room door, a neighbor, Spargo, posted "Sir".

The last I will recall here was Lynn Pagliaro. He had been dating a girl named Maureen whenever he went home for breaks. During one Visitors Day, Maureen's parents came by to have a look at (and judge) their daughter's new boyfriend. In this way I got to guide a very stern looking Ronald Reagan and wife to Lynn's room. Unlike most of us, Lynn was remarkably mature for his age, measured, thoughtful, and even distinguished. Clear to me that he would be very successful in his life. Maybe not so to Ronald Reagan though. Not sure how it all worked out at the time. Even Death Valley might have smelled much better for Reagan than our own swell dormitory home.

Photo B. Clarkson College faculty were, if nothing else, undeterred by the bone chilling cold. A hardy lot, many had arrived from equally chilly or desolate places elsewhere on the globe.

This is a photo of our Economics Professor. From Switzerland, he spritzed substantially and with impressive range, when he lectured. The students were huddling in the last rows of the classroom, one with an umbrella as I recall, but the lecturer continued on oblivious.

Photos C, D, E. The death of hazing: Clarkson's generational secret emerges.

The hazing of freshmen by sophomores was continuing month after month with no end in sight. Freshmen could be ordered to streak without clothes from one dormitory building to another. This was a short run but at 40 degrees below zero risked pneumonia, certainly some respiratory damage. Freshman could have their head shaved for disobedience. In a good day, they would at least be stopped routinely and harassed. We got the freshman to walk in groups of five or six to or from class. It felt more like High School than College.

The few law enforcement individuals were nowhere to be found once summer ended. Rumor had it that they were "Snowbirds" migrating to warmer Florida to leave the snow behind. So a lawless place with little recourse.

Except for the one that needed to be realized. A secret passed on through the generations. I knew what it was. Should I announce it on my weekly one-hour radio show? Was the time right? Why not? This had gone on long enough.

On my next show: *"Have you ever noticed that the sophomores returning this year are a lot fewer than last year? They are down to less than 300 now. This means the freshmen class at more than 500 outnumbers them. So why is hazing continuing so long? Let it fill the whole year? Notice that no stop date has ever been given by the College? Here is the Clarkson secret passed on down through generations of hazing. It stops when the freshmen SAY it's over! That's all it takes. We just declare it done and it's done. Then the College gives us a little weekend ceremony to end it traditionally. How about it? Is it done?"*

Back at the dorm signs saying HAZING IS OVER were everywhere. So it ended then and there.

Except for that College ceremony promised for the next weekend to come. Fine for the freshmen to declare hazing over. For the sophomores a more vivid experience was called for to make their new situation clear and final. A ceremony was designed for exactly that.

The sophomore 300 lined up on one end of the football field and the freshman 500 on the other end. In the middle was a huge canvas ball. Officially the rules were to push the ball into the opposing goal posts. But with no referees to be seen that day (true to the Potsdam and College spirit of the times), 800 males met in the middle, more or less where the ball was, and conflict ensued. This blew off steam, followed by a more relaxed campus situation. Some bruises and bandages but no fatalities (a gentler time). They all moved on. This is what photographs C-E captured.

In my second year I tipped off the freshmen after just one week of hazing. They organized quickly. Hazing ended the second week, a Clarkson record.

Some of my classmates were not happy about this. They had looked forward to getting even with their oppressors from last year by taking it out on the new students this year. Way to pass on sadism over generations, prophetic of Eduardo Duran's intergenerational trauma insights so many decades later.

Well, I was against hazing then and I am against it now. Phil Zimbardo has shown how bad this inequity can get. On the other hand: *When* and *How* the hazing stopped was a rite of passage for Clarkson students. They gained the maturity of learning their own power to make change, to protect themselves by group action when no adult force was there to do it for them. Sure enough, those passing through this ritual seemed to mature substantially. More self-sufficient, more independent critical thinkers. Less likely to succumb to dysfunctional authority. Very useful for citizens in our challenging world of today.

Photo F. Our Army ROTC marching stroll every Thursday.

We were scheduled for the Army ROTC training our first two years though an equal time of Physical Education (PE) could be substituted. Out of curiosity I stayed with ROTC. Turned out a very Clarkson/Potsdam approach to the Army. The commanding officer was Colonel Clarence Campbell. He later ran the pro hockey league, a big sport in snow country. But back in the late 1950s, the Colonel was more of a front lines kind of leader. He made sure we knew how to shoot, how to do the manual of arms hefting the surplus M-1 we carried. It felt as heavy as I was.

As to precision marching, he had disdain for that. Didn't think it would keep us alive in a shooting situation. So we marched as in coming back from the Front. When most are not in step, synchrony disappears. See photo F. Individuation very much in literal step with the Clarkson/Potsdam (CP: opposite of PC) spirit. I marched, more or less, the first year. The second year I drew on my High School newspaper editor experience and offered to be the photographer and press liaison. The Colonel agreed. A very good man, that Campbell. The second year no more marching with M-1s every Thursday. I just hefted my camera.

A few years later, in the time of impending draft, I was in the USAF Officer Training or OTS. They assumed my Potsdam marching experience with ROTC was a plus. I did prove true to my Clarkson CP experience, marching at shifting cadences and directions when it intuitively suited my legs. Too boring for these legs to conform indefinitely to what everybody else was doing. Did not go over well though.

I did eventually get to Hawaii where I did my postdoc clinical internship.

After leaving Potsdam, it still took me six years to get there.

Meals without Wheels (1959)

Themes: *The Great Pretender* Platters; *Fun* Sly & the Family Stone

The Trip

Doug Griffin, a past college roommate, forwarded this memory to me from a friend from that long ago era. All I recall now from this holiday trip from Potsdam to Buffalo was that the hole in the floor of the car gave a fresh view of the road we were traveling on as we progressed.

> *"Dear Doug,*
>
> *Doug were you part of the group going back to Clarkson after Christmas break in Jim Lepsch's old Plymouth? The old car that did not have a heater nor a defroster; so that in a snow storm one had to drive with some window open. Well Bob Morgan was part of the crew of four or five. After Syracuse the snow storm got quite strong. It was getting dark and some of us were afraid of ending up in a ditch. It was decided that the next time we saw a hotel or motel we would stop for the night. So we stopped at an old hotel in some tiny town in Northern New York in a snow storm. The quoted price was maybe $65 each or maybe $80. So Bob says, "Let's see what happens when we appeal to the compassion of the folks who live here. We will knock on doors and say we are*

poor college students caught in a storm with no money for the hotel (all true). So can you put us up for one night?" Well it seemed like a good plan to 19 year old students. There was a small green in that town and we went to about 8 houses around that green. There were no offers of hospitality. We than came upon a house that looked like a share croppers. It has a low porch between it and the sidewalk. It lacked paint. Light streaming out its big front window, which was not the well-insulated type seen in New York State. It was clearly a home for a low income family. I am pretty sure there was a fireplace and a roaring fire inside and the place was crowded with happy people. So we knocked. They swallowed us up with kindness. They helped us warm up and then gave us bacon and eggs to eat. They did not have room for us due to the number of their quests. But they told us where their pastor lived. We tried the pastor's door. The pastor had a grand house. We may have said the generous people down the street sent us here. The pastor and his family looked as us askance. But did us up for the night. And served us a nice breakfast the next day. As I recall, an icy air hung over the table. I was embarrassed then and am still embarrassed. But Bob Morgan loved it."

Arthur and Larry (1960-1962)

Maybe that earlier trip was the beginning of this pattern. Meals without wheels.

In 1960 I transferred into Michigan State University (MSU) for my last two under-graduate years, this time as a new psychology major.

The first year there we were obligated to stay in a dormitory. Mine was reserved for keeping bad influences away from the younger first year students fresh from high school. That was university defined as older transfers like me, returning military, discipline problems, and international students. So there was the great luck, being in the most creative multi-cultural multi-racial nonconforming MSU dorm location there was that year.

Top novelist Tom McGuane was there, also a paratrooper who loved to jump from his fourth floor window, past my second floor one, on to the rolling hills below, a few highly amusing alcoholics, some super athletes (eg. Hockey), and students from all over the world.

As before, Arthur was my roommate for most of this time. From Bermuda, he looked much like a younger beefier Malcolm X. Arthur played Soccer, headed the campus model United Nations, and played Bid Whist cards with our Detroit friends every Sunday.

I soon learned that Bermudians had some unique words and accents, still in the King's English, but far from the Midwest pronunciations found in Michigan. Gave me an idea.

Our second year at MSU, my last as an undergraduate, we were free from the dorms, and their excellent cafeteria food. So, along with our friends, we moved into cheap town rentals. Food though was now a problem. Few of us had much money.

A day's meal at times might have been the 25 cent hamburger at that brand new fast food chain, *McDonalds*.

This would not do.

Time for my plan.

We put up notices all over town like this:

Share Your Dinner with a Foreign Student Guest
(Interpreter will accompany)

And a local number from a favorite hangout.

A few takers were all we needed and their invitations did come in.

Arthur borrowed an African Dashiki from Larry, another of our past dorm pals. Larry was from Ghana.

Arthur showed up at a welcome dinner in his African garb and I translated. This involved a few Bermudian words like "*dickty*", meaning "*goofy*" or in Michigan parlance "*Not really pleasant*". I added a few cooking specialties involving sugar and salt on chicken. But mostly, Arthur just spoke plain English and then I would translate with cultural anecdotes, traditions, mating patterns, and, maybe, a few stretched possibilities that came to mind. Arthur struggled to keep a straight face during all this but managed in the end to smile rather than laugh. After dinner, we collected our borrowed Bermudian flag and left to applause, satiated by a great meal.

Larry soon joined our effort as the foreign student from Ghana. He was in fact from the capital, Accra, and was very sophisticated. Still, once in his Dashiki, and a bone over his nose, he was the very expectation of local dinner hosts who assumed he was fresh from an African jungle. Larry loved this and in fact gave me many cultural inserts to translate. Though Larry, as did Arthur, spoke perfect English the entire dinner.

Of many delicious courses.

After

Once we graduated, Arthur had a Rhodes scholarship to study economics in Europe but with a stop on the way in Cuba. There he spent a few weeks with Cuba's Economics Minister, Che Guevera.

Now, Arthurs years of waiting had ended and he had his invitation to speak at the United Nations. The timing came just after the end of his Rhodes experience and was perfect for him. Arthur's minority party in Bermuda had to choose between ignoring this opportunity or letting the young recent graduate represent his country. They chose the second option.

Arthur spoke eloquently at the UN for his country's independence from Great Britain. In the dorm he had drawn me out often about why my country wanted no monarchy. He enjoyed this debate, asking, for example, why we wouldn't want this living reminder of our past. For that, I asked him if he would want to keep his burst appendix on his mantle to honor its memory. Arthur found a way to use some of these remarks in his address.

Still, even after all these many years, Bermuda is still part of the British Empire, though with reduced compliance. And Arthur is now a retired Bermudian judge, also still of little compliance.

We lost touch with Larry, who returned to Accra after his graduation.

It is reasonable to assume he left his over-the-nose bone behind him in Michigan.

Back in his home country his dinner invitations would have no need for an interpreter any more.

Sight Unseen

Theme: *The Old Lamplighter* Ed Brown and the Browns

Buffalo, New York. World War II was over.

The East side of the city where we lived was changing from pockets of Eastern Europeans to majority African-Americans up from the South. South Buffalo residents were largely Polish and German communities. The city's West side was a fast growing Italian community. Of these, Sicilian immigrants dominated.

My mother, as a young woman, had taught many West side children. Her salary went mostly to her parents and their children, 14 in all. Living frugally, she still loved her work. And the students loved her back as did their parents.

As a child I recall her taking me to visit one particular family there. The mother, by then a grandmother, spoke no English but she always rushed to greet us with a *"Teach!"* and a hug. Her two boys, Tony and Marty, were now grown with families of their own but they were always there to greet us as well. Marty was gruff but sentimental. Tony, the elder, was always polished and considerate.

Marty ran a detective agency. He was respected from a distance, sometimes with what seemed like fear.

Tony was now Anthony, an attorney, and was liked by everyone he met. He exuded a quiet professional confidence. If he took your case, you know all would be well.

When I got to be 21, I retained Anthony to help a woman with three children get divorced. So I could marry her. He was effective and relentlessly kind. Always a breath of fresh air.

I was told that they both were Mafioso. Anthony was said to be a Consigliere.

In the Buffalo of the 1940s, especially on its West side, the Mafia was often respected and, by many, appreciated. They kept crime to a minimum and I heard often then that they were an essential community resource.

It was so much a community feature that I clearly remember that one of the neighborhood baseball teams was called the *"Mafia Juniors"*. This was the name on their uniforms. This title was not tongue-in-cheek.

Then again, the later 1950s and 1960s would bring a very different perspective.

In his own later years, Anthony began losing his vision. He got the best doctors but the prognosis was unanimous. His cataracts were expanding. He would be blind in about a year. They had no treatment for this then.

Anthony withdrew his savings and closed his practice. All of it.

He and his wife spent the year seeing the world together while he could see at all. Romantic. Tragic.

As predicted, by the end of that year, he no longer could see.

And then his doctors were happy to tell him that a new surgery had become available, one to remove the cataracts from his eyes and restore his sight.

It worked.

His family rejoiced, his community celebrated.

But he had no money or job left.

So: He began his life anew, from scratch.

It turned out to be even better than before.

After

His brother Marty had made a success out of a detective agency and tided his brother over until his practice resumed.

Which it did quickly, considering.

Rosie DeMatteo was eventually the matriarch of her own large family, also our friends. I think it was her great granddaughter Drea that played a role in the *Sopranos* television series.

Anthony's practice with his community thrived. His brother Marty had a role also and was much respected or feared as the case would be. Terms like "consigliere" or "enforcer" may have been applied to the brothers but never in *our* house.

My mother went to a West Side dinner honoring her, along with her husband.

My father was asked to make some remarks.

He thanked them for their warm welcome, great food, and long friendship.

Then he added that they were unfairly linked to all those dangerous Sicilian Mafia thugs reviled in the press, those that were hurting the good name of the rest of our Italian citizens.

He said his wife whispered to him when he sat down that they were *all* in fact Sicilian Mafia families. He had had no idea of this and it was too late now.

My father smiled when telling this story. Nothing bad had happened to him.

Their respect for my mother probably made the difference.

I can imagine Marty Moscato being whispered to by his sister Rosie and his older brother Anthony: *"Let it slide"*.

1960s

Gerber's Picante Sauce, Love, & Tie-dye

LOVE IS BLIND

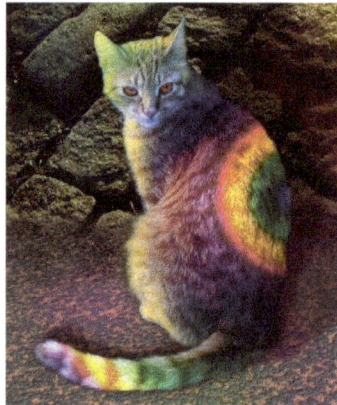

How You Know

Topic: If She Is *Really* Into You

When you see her in the distance, you make an outstandingly loud farting noise.

She stops, turns toward you.

You do it again, even louder and longer.

Next you yell *"That was my mating call!"*

Now she runs toward you, fast.

Yes! It worked! She passed the test. She's a **keeper**! Then-

Room to move
Becky Owl and Craig Menteer perform a modern dance at a Friday afternoon

Maybe not. He landed a record 12 yards away.

Falling Leaves

Theme: *Autumn Leaves* Nat King Cole/
Paula Cole

Autumn trees on the Red Cedar River at Michigan State University.

This is such a popular place for temporary or spontaneous romance that anything thrown into the river will bounce back from the rubber-strewn river bed.

Or so it is said.

Canadian Suzanne Simard (2021) in her long study of mother trees suddenly realized that they were exhibiting real intelligence.

This included the selective reserving and distributing of water to other trees that were family or friends.

Books by German ecologist Peter Wohlleben (2018, 2019), translated into English, share that autumn leaves change to beautiful colors as a process of dying.

Before they drop, the tree fills each of them with discarded waste as a process of defecation.

Drawing from his national culture's legendary sense of high humor and delicate wit, he tells us that dropped autumn leaves are "*the tree's toilet paper*".

No translator error here, but possibly the seasonal insight to remember.

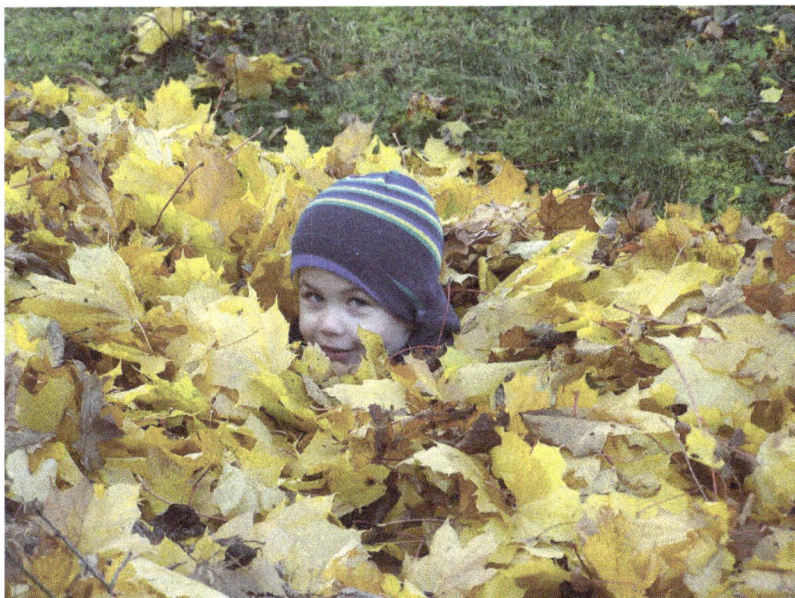

Have a great fall season.

Revisit this moment any time in the year.

Larry and Terry

Theme: *Love Tastes like Strawberries* Miriam Makeba;

1960-1962 Michigan State University (MSU)

Larry

Theme: *I Scare Myself* Dan Hicks and the Hot Licks

Larry had just turned thirty. He looked into the bathroom mirror, seeing a tall bearded man. A worried man. Just a year away from his doctorate in anthropology, career uncertain.

In his generation, turning 30 was seen as entering into old age, a downward slope to sure and certain disability followed by death.

He knew better but it gave him pause.

And what about Hilda?

Hilda was a professor in the Creative Writing department. She also owned the house where Larry had rented a room. That was two years ago now.

Once moved in, Larry was delighted to find that his time with Hilda each evening was the best part of his rental. She was kind, witty, supportive, insightful, affectionate, and attractive.

Even though she was almost 30 years older than Larry, he felt he had found his soulmate.

Larry recalled his favorite fiction author, Robert Heinlein, pointing out that only with the passage of many years did anybody's 'true face' appear.

He realized that Hilda's true face was elegant, beautiful.

In time they slept together as well, felt like a couple.

Hilda was clear that she understood the barrier of the years between them.

Not a barrier to her but to most everybody else, doubly so for those tolerating a May-December romance. Okay if it was the man that was December, but impossible if the older partner was a woman.

So they just kept their privacy and enjoyed the time together day by day by day. Or rather night by night.

Still. Lately Larry, despite his setting aside the cultural disapproval of their age gap, began drifting apart whenever they had sex.

Hilda told him that he was very satisfying as a lover.

But telling her of his drift during sex might hurt her or so he thought.

Finally, in their time together one night, he chose to trust her with the truth. To his surprise, she took it very well.

Said it happens in most relationships eventually. Since this sexual issue was the only challenge their age difference caused, how might they get past it?

At last, Hilda said he just needed some better visualizations during their intimacy. She wasn't his keeper.

Maybe he should have some one-night stands with a woman his age, and see if it helps.

This didn't sit well with Larry.

But he promised he would consider it.

Sat with me in the Kewpees restaurant the next day, as his friend, and shared his dilemma fully.

Following his lead, I promised I would 'consider it' and get back to him.

Kewpees

Theme: *Spinning Wheel* Blood, Sweat, and Tears

That year Kewpees was still there, the hangout at the edge of the campus.

MSU was very diverse, international students abounded that year. Still, the largest bunches of on-campus students clustered in two groups: (1) Jocks and their athletic supporters, and (2) the arts & crafts crowd. There was little or no communication between these groups. A cousin I grew up with was in the first group in all my time there but I never knew of him until after he graduated. I was in the second group and frequented the gathering spot for these at this place called Kewpees.

Kewpees was a coffee shop and bar with decent comfort food. Its many tables filled at night with university patrons, fresh from the movies or live theater or cramming for an exam with no witnesses.

Some of us did all our course reading and writing on the weekend during football games, times when the library was desolate and available. This led to many evenings free of responsibility to discourse at Kewpees.

The manager of Kewpees was a fixture. He sat by the phone on his desk at a place of honor behind the bar. A gentleman, he would answer any call and then, via his microphone, announce the name that was sought for the call. As you might imagine, should you be like those of us at the tables, many calls were bogus. Yet the manager relayed them without censure: *"Call for Tom Jefferson; Tom you are wanted on the phone!"* Or *"Call for Mike Hunt. Mike Hunt needed here!"* Laughter or applause as the case might have been. He was either a great sport or just our great sport. Either way, a night at Kewpees.

At the close of the next day, I sat there with two couples, none of them students, all in their early twenties like me.

Dark Carnival (DC) had a job at MSU's art department as a nude model. He was finely muscled, red hair, and looked like a young Kirk Douglas. DC was born as Bill Gribbon but, fresh from Canada, he wanted us to call him *"Dark Carnival"*, a title from the first book of short stories by Ray Bradbury. DC had a great sense of humor. An instant friend.

DC was with Belle, an intense woman with dark hair to go with his *Dark Carnival* identity. She seemed decades wiser than her age, a warm maturity somewhat striking. Bobbie Gentry or Loretta Lynn could have played her in any biopic movie about Belle.

Dick looked very much his age, smiling easily, woodsy, in his case looking much like a young Kris Kristofferson. With him sat Terry.

Terry's body owned the word *"voluptuous."* As what was once said of actor Robert Mitchum, her chest entered the room before she did. Her brown hair was cut short, her eyes violet like Liz Taylor, her expression both happy and sultry. Terry, born as Taiisa, claimed to be from a royal German family, now living in Michigan. She worshipped Marlene Dietrich records as her own theme music. Terry was engaged to marry Dick.

We were all instant friends. At the time I was a graduate student in psychology and a beginning writer. My favorite pen pal was the very Ray Bradbury that DC idolized.

(Bradbury and another Sci Fi author, Fritz Leiber, had been very encouraging, always responsive. I took a creative writing class one term led by an instructor named Justin Leiber. When I asked, he said that Fritz was his father. So I was happy to give him one of my best fresh new stories as the first class assignment. He gave it a C+, saying it was "over opulent". Much like his dad's Swords and Deviltry series with hyper-opulent adventure heroes Fafhrd and the Gray Mouser? Well, I toned it down and passed the class. My first book came out the next year with a great jacket endorsement from Fritz.")

(And then Justin did a decent book on the imagined anthropomorphic life of our immunizing armies of white blood cells. Straight forward and not over-opulent.)

My time that first day with the two couples ended on this exchange:

Dick: *"You know, Terry's parents don't approve of me at all. They say 'What kind of life will she ever have if we get married?' As we plan to do. Her mother said 'Live in the forest on nuts and berries?' "*

DC: *"So Terry. What do you plan to say to your parents the next time this comes up?"*

Belle: *"Yes! Let them know why you chose him. What is the truth exactly?"*

Terry: *"Simple. I LOVE DICK!"*

Laughter from Belle, DC, and those at the tables next to them. Terry had been loud with her emphatic declaration.

Dick just grinned and nodded.

DC: *"Honest. But you might not want to put it that way."*

Belle agreed.

But Terry in her emphasis and wording had brought out a key worry.

Terry and Her Admirers

Theme: *Great Balls of Fire* Jerry Lee Lewis

I had an apartment in married housing although my fiancé was months late in joining me. Alone, I was still busy with classes and a dozen temporary university jobs.

Both local couples visited from time to time.

And then Terry began regular solo visits. She seemed to think I already had clinical psychology training, which I had not yet, though as a friend, I was good at keeping secrets and kept hers. (Until now.) Terry was naturally seductive but I honored my doomed marital commitment to another woman, a fiancé not yet arrived, and eventually she relaxed.

One bright sunny day she stopped by to share some photographs of herself. She had filled in for DC to nude model at the art department and had been rewarded with her own set of nude photos. Impressive, sure. Maybe a little too eager to view these with me. In my response, I was complimentary. How else?

She left to get a routine checkup for her car. Put the photos in an envelope in her glove compartment. Walked away and shopped for the afternoon until it was time to get her car back.

On arrival, about half a dozen mechanics were there to greet her, all smiling widely. She returned their attentions with a smile, used to this level of male responsiveness. Only when she got home, did she realize her envelope of nude photographs was missing from the glove compartment.

She came to visit me the next day to share the event and consider responses. She ruled out telling Dick as he might think she had wanted this attention. Decided in the end to get another set of her photos from the art department and otherwise forget about it. She admitted some excitement about all her new fans at the garage.

I suggested she might consider her relationship with her fiancé as the trust needed for a marriage can be damaged by withholding secrets that they would each expect from the other. She said she would think on it.

Much of my free time was spent in a large room set aside for psychology graduate students. One afternoon I was reading in the room when Terry walked in.

That day all the inhabitants were male. All perked up when Terry arrived. Ignoring them, she walked up to me and asked to speak privately. About a request. Well, I would have had to go somewhere else for that and was just an hour short of finishing the reading. So I asked if she needed privacy or could just visit me here and now.

She turned to the dozen males with me and said *"Are you all in psychology?"* All their own work set aside, they raptly nodded yes.

"Okay then. This can't wait. I am only speaking to Robert but you can listen in if you're as good as he is at honoring confidential secrets. I mean that whatever I say to him, you keep it to yourself." All nodded yes again.

"Robert. The only man I have ever had sex with is Dick. I realize that means I can't know for sure if he is the man I should marry without ever having the experience of sex first with another man. Maybe my attraction to him is mostly sexual, not enough for a lifetime together. But this needs to be with somebody I can absolutely trust. With you. Will you come to my house tomorrow afternoon? My parents are gone for the day. Will you have sex with me?"

Involuntary quiet groans from two guys in the room.

I said no. (Fresh groans of disbelief from the students in the room. Their own eager volunteer offers she ignored.)

But I told her I had a better idea.

Sometimes two problems can solve each other.

Larry with Terry

Theme: *I'm Tired* (Blazing Saddles movie) Madeline Kahn

As we walked away from the building. I told her about Larry. He was only a little older than Dick, just as good looking, and in addition his last name was of German origin. He would be discreet about their rendezvous and never see her again. She was enthusiastic. Took his contact information and arranged it for that afternoon.

Late that evening Larry met with me at Kewpees. Described his adventure. Terry had brought him directly to her bedroom. Pink little girl decoration, large four poster bed, Marlene Dietrich posters. They removed their clothes and Larry was momentarily happy at this vision. But then he had to listen to an hour, or it seemed an hour, of many Marlene Dietrich records.

The sex did then happen and that part appeared to be good for each of them. But just good, not great. An after-sex conversation was attempted but trailed off soon, as they had so little in common.

Larry with Hilda

Theme: *Sometimes Like a River* Joy of Cooking

Larry said he realized now that he actually loved Hilda. No substitute would do.

His sex with her might improve if he let himself be guided and powered by that love, not performance.

Being open to Hilda's clues might better please both of them. They could develop silent signs for *"more please"* or *"move on"*.

And so it was.

By the time I graduated, Larry and Hilda had come out to their friends as a couple.

To welcome and approval.

They were the happiest couple I knew.

After

Theme: *Junk Food Junkie* Larry Groce

I lost track of DC and Belle but hope to see them again someday. Terry did marry her Dick. They moved to central California where the Redwood trees lived. And where both nuts and berries were abundant.

Closing Note

Theme: *Only Time Will Tell Me* Joy of Cooking

> *"Here is a new day, fresh, untouched. What will you do with it?"*
>
> -Native American Church prayer

Often those in Chinese culture avoid speaking of death as that might invite it.

In my Singapore lifespan seminar, the psychology graduate students that had been raised in that culture, found the phase of life with death impending hard to discuss.

Though, for their future patients, they took the risk. In Japanese culture the opposite can be found.

There an awareness of one's sure and certain death can be used to energize appreciation of life. While we have it.

Those friends we have along the way seem to live in our memory as vivid time statues, eternally on higher ground.

Eventually we and they must leave our world for the destination below the ground.

Hold this awareness and now fully cherish the time we have.

Closing Theme: *Closer to the Ground* Joy of Cooking

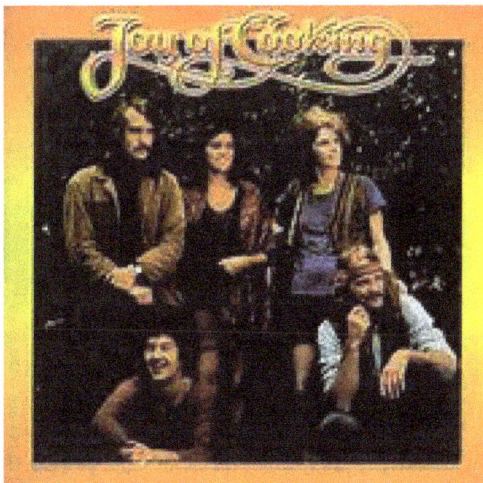

Chirp

Themes: *When the Saints Go Marching In* Howard Gospel Choir; *Hold on I'm Coming* Eric Clapton · B.B. King · David Porter, Isaac Hayes, Sam & Dave; *War: What is it good for? Absolutely Nothing* Edwin Starr

This was the day when one in **Big Red** *would meet the little death.*

1962 USAF Base, San Antonio, Texas.

In the time of the invasion of Viet Nam, I was a Staff Sergeant (4 stripes) in the USAF Officer Training or OTS.

The trainers assumed my marching experience with ROTC was a plus. I did prove true to my prior *Madstop* chapter experience, marching at shifting cadences and directions when it intuitively suited my legs. Too boring for these legs to conform indefinitely to what everybody else was doing. Did not go over well though.

A friend from high school, Bill, was doing the same in California. He finished his training and started his military life as a second lieutenant. The ones over the hill first and most likely to be shot immediately. Bill may well have taken this into consideration before he was flown out of the country into Viet Nam combat. I heard he had been marching his platoon along a path paralleling a drop off to a river on the platoon's left. Ordered them to double time and then bellowed the order *"Left Turn NOW!"* They all obeyed. Nobody drowned but it was a really wet uniform day.

At the court martial, Bill shared his amazement that they had obeyed him. He said that he had just been curious as to whether any of them could think for themselves fast and on their feet.

Curiosity fulfilled, Bill was sent home without an honorable discharge. But still alive. A legend in his own mind, and dry.

Back at the base in Texas, our own military training was also to obey orders: in the moment and without second thoughts.

For some of us, we took time for that consideration later.

Each division of our trainees was assigned a fictitious marching mascot. Ours was *Big Red*- an 800 pound canary.

We marched in a four-step cadence. For us, the *Big Red One*, on every fourth step we yelled our loudest: *"CHIRP!"*

The drill sergeant noticed we were not as fully focused on this march as he thought we should be. He told us to practice on our own: *"Take a moment while in full stride to think of a very powerful distraction. Then overcome it and keep marching in perfect step. Until you can ignore the distraction so completely you march through it!"*

I went out to a marching spot when nobody else was there. Took a practice circuit. All in step.

Second loop coming up. Being only 21 and now long away from feminine company, I summoned an erotic memory. Was okay to set it to the side, let it play, as I was marching just fine.

Felt the sensation growing. Let it grow. I would keep marching. And did.

For a few more steps.

An orgasm was due any second. I would march through it.

It came. I came. My body was frozen in mid stride.

A frozen second.

The French call it *"La Petite Mort"* or the little death.

Sounds much better than the word *"orgasm"*, yes?

And then, my marching resumed.

I had just learned that it is impossible to march, or move, while having an orgasm. Important to know for marching troops everywhere. My military contribution.

Well, what would the giant **red canary** expect of me now?

I bellowed *"CHIRP!"*

Some distant heads turned.

I swooped back to the barracks to change clothes.

Afterthought from Psychologist Dr. Gene Orro, WWII Vet

His invited Memorial Day Tribute remarks:

> *"As the search for peace remains in vain*
> *The thought of war and heroes gives me pain*
> *So I dare to be so rude*
> *As to wish the ants your picnic food*
> *And pray the clouds obscure our sun with shade*
> *And rain water, cats, and dogs, on your parade."*

This was read at his own funeral memorial not long after.

Rollo May and the Earthworm

Theme: *Closer to the Ground* Joy of Cooking

Two of the most brilliant mentors I've ever known met each other only once and then that only for a few memorable seconds.

It was about 1964. I was a graduate student in psychology.

My great good luck was to be supervised in my very first psychology class by Stanley C. Ratner. He looked like Basil Rathbone's dignified version of Sherlock Holmes. Calm and clear he always was, with a subtle but insightful sense of humor. Officially a psychologist he was really a naturalist, a great admirer of the full range of animal life. He shared with me once that he had only seen the Bambi movie as an adult, but cried when Bambi's mother was killed by a hunter. (Disney held little back from children in their beginning.) Stan was much admired, respected, trusted by the other department faculty.

Though they were often puzzled by his choice of which animal he had chosen to study. He had written the full spectrum textbook of the animal kingdom. But now he was studying ... *earthworms*. He let this ride in the department without any excessive explanation. But to me, he shared that he wanted to learn the most about vertebrates, including humans, and had decided to begin his education with the simplest animal having a central nervous system- *Lumbricus Terrestris*, our friendly neighborhood worm.

One day we had a very distinguished guest speaker for our weekly gathering of faculty and grad students. Filled a small auditorium. Student attendance was voluntary, but we were there in large numbers. It was Rollo May, a very famous expert in Existential Psychology, a fresh perspective that included *"situational ethics"*. This was highly interesting to young randy scholars in a very specific practical way since it encouraged in-context spontaneity in sexual relationships, absent the straitjacket of outdated constraints.

Of course, Rollo introduced us to much more in his talk.

Including bringing existential philosophy into psychology to guide our lifetime. Existential in today's language has come to mean a life threatening issue. The original deeper meaning was the lens from which we made sense of the world we navigated. A way of knowing that, in psychology, could be used to improve or heal those who came to us for help.

Coming from Sartre's post-WW2 philosophy, it dealt with understanding our human existence with each other. And, as philosophy, it valued the question even more than its answer.

Back to Rollo May's talk that day. Ending his lecture, it was time for him to take questions from the audience.

Stan Ratner stood up and asked the first question. We all wondered what our most distinguished teacher or colleague would ask this celebrity.

Ratner said *"How does Existentialism apply to earthworms?"*

The audience fell very silent. Rollo considered this for a moment.

Then he replied with clear sincerity: *"THAT is a very interesting question."*

And moved on to the next question.

Years later Rollo, godfather to my daughters, didn't recall this.

Stan was no longer around to ask.

For me, I had learned that simple honesty is a very good answer.

The Prophecy

Theme: *"A Change is Gonna Come"* Sam Cooke

The Lost Generation finding their way

Early entering the 1960s. To push back against school desegregation in Virginia, Prince Edward County, an entire school system was closed for its Black children.

For years.

When federal intervention finally reopened those schools, the children were placed in grades by their age. This meant that the first cohort of high school graduates that was going to college would be missing years of their education.

They were termed the *"lost generation"* in the press.

The missing school years had depressed their tested IQ scores, as compared to similar children in a neighboring county.

That's how it was proved that the Tested IQ used in schools in that day actually depended on prior education. It was not particularly genetic as usually measured.

Analyzing learning deficits based on the age children had suffered from closed schools, we found critical ages for skill in reading and math. Potentially, without help, a lifelong handicap.

A federal grant through the US Office of Education was launched with the goal to bring this *"lost generation"* up to speed before these children began their higher education.

A large cohort of dedicated teachers signed on to attempt this jump of years in a single summer.

Dr. Robert Lee Green was in charge of this program, including the before and after evaluation of both these students and their summer teachers.

As Bob's graduate student associate, I took on the assessment of the teacher cohort.

The large group of teachers began their own pre-training that summer by assembling for the first time in a testing room with a demographic form to fill out.

They began.

Most were of the same race as their intended students though here and there were a few different faces. One of those with a white face raced his hand.

He looked to be in his early twenties, much like me.

I acknowledged him.

He said *"I see you want us to list our race here. Why do you want us to do that?*

I answered *"Sure. Understanding why anybody would ask a question like that is important. In our case, we need to prove to the grant provider that we have a racially diverse group here. This is a deseg-regation effort."*

He frowned and said *"I object! I don't see race. We are all just human here."*

By now the whole room's occupants had put down their pens and were paying attention. A few looked at this young man with concern.

I had to get things back on track. Not for the teachers. Then and always for the students.

"Yes, far as I can tell, we are all of the same human family. Now look around the room and also see the beauty of this rainbow of skin tones. We are here because the School Board has damaged your soon-to-be students because of discrimination against their non-white shades. Children held back from their better future by the School Board's ignorance. We are here now to do something helpful for those children, now young adults going to college. Something valuable."

But the indignant volunteer teacher wasn't about to quit.

"Well, I'm telling you right now. I'm not going to write a race down here for me on this paper! For me it will stay blank."

I thought sure, his tell-tale blank would be as white as he was. But he meant well.

I just responded with: *"That's your right. Go ahead and leave it blank then. As to race, when I collect your completed form, I'll just make a wild guess."*

The teachers went back to completing their evaluation forms.

After drowning me in a sea of smiles.

After

The best question I asked on the evaluation form was to ask what percentage of their students would, by the end of the summer program, test at the educational level of children ready to begin college.

The results were significant, statistically and psychologically. Each teacher's class progress matched closely with their own predicted percentages. A Robert Rosenthal and Lenore Jacobson self-fulfilling prophecy effect: A teacher's positive belief in their ability can enhance their student's progress. Their learning. Their better future.

In the summer project results, the same happened. When a teacher expected good results, their students mostly succeeded at that level. Or: low teacher expectations of their students were matched by low student outcomes.

How else did the children do?

By the end of the summer program, as a whole cohort, they had advanced substantially in their readiness.

Most though had not caught up fully for all the lost school years. The college challenge to come would test them sorely.

Once the cohort had finished their time in college, those who made it to graduation were best predicted by one factor. A psychological measure.

Their motivation to succeed.

Those who cared the most, those who believed they would prevail, they stayed the course. They got to the finish line.

And the better life beyond.

Did these graduates get some success experiences from a teacher that believed in them back then in that early pre-college summer?

Looked to us that the children got to follow what had become their own self-fulfilling prophecy.

Sources

Green, R.L., Morgan, R.F., and Hoffman, L.J. (1970) 'Effects of deprivation on ntelligence, achievement, & cognitive growth." In Robert Wilcox (Ed), Chapter One, *The Psychological Consequences of Being a Black American: Research by Black Psychologists.* New York: Wiley.

Green R.L. & Morgan, R,F. (1970) "The effects of resumed schooling on the measured intelligence of Prince Edward County's Black children." In Roger Wilcox (Ed.), *The Psychological Consequences of Being a Black American: Research by Black Psychologists..* New York: Wiley.

Green, R. L. & Morgan, R.F. (1969) "Compensatory education and educational growth." In Robert L. Green (Ed.), *Racial Crisis in American Education.* Chicago: Follett, 1969. Chapter 9: Pp. 186-219.

Green, R.L. & Morgan, R.F. (1969) Effects of resumed schooling on the measured intelligence of Prince Edward County's black children. *Journal of Negro Education, 38,* 147-155.

Green, R.L., Morgan, R.F., and Hoffman, L.J. (1967) Effects of deprivation on intelligence, achievement, and cognitive growth: A review. *Journal of Negro Education, 36,* 5-14.

Green, R.L., Morgan, R.F., Hoffman, L.J., Morse, R.J., Hayes, M. (1964) *Educational Status of Children in a District without Public Schools: CRP 3221.* Washington, D.C.: United States Office of Education, 1964.

Green, R.L., Morgan, R.F., Hoffman, L.J., Morse, R.J. (1964) *The Educational Status of Children during the First Year Following Four Years of Little or No Schooling: CRP 2498.* Washington, D.C.; United States Office of Education, 1964.

Rosenthal, R. & Jacobson, L. (2003) *Pygmalion in the Classroom: Teacher Expectation and Pupils' Intellectual Development Expanded Edition.* New York: Crown House. (Prior editions in 1968 and in 1992).

Turtles, Dogs, and Eagles

Themes: *You've got to be Carefully Taught (South Pacific)* Rodgers & Hammerstein; *Stairway to Heaven* Led Zeppelin

Some 50+ years ago, my graduate psychology classroom in Nova Scotia, Canada was fully decorated with the art of second graders.

The young artists had been separated two years earlier into three class groups. This division was primarily based on IQ test scores. Although the children were not told their own scores or which group was high or low, they could guess. The groups were named after animals: Eagles, Dogs, and Turtles. There were a few exceptions to the IQ as a basis for this assignment: some of the children from wealthier or more influential families, despite modest IQ scores, were assigned to the Eagles, while some of the High IQ core children who had challenging behavior were assigned to the Turtles.

Two years later, a new Grade 2 art teacher was working with these children. She saw herself as quite progressive in that past art teachers had taught all children from the same formula while she had adapted her methods to the perceived differences of the ability of the three groups. She was eager to share her results with my university students and the results sat on our wall.

The Eagles had been given a wide variety of art supplies and had been asked to do a winter scene. She then consulted with each child artist as requested until all the young artists had finished their work. The wall in my classroom set aside for the resulting artwork of the Eagles was ablaze with color and talent, reflecting the creative atmosphere the artist had enjoyed.

The Dogs on the other hand, were not asked to create a winter scene, but more specifically to copy a snowman the teacher drew for them on the board. Each young artist was given a piece of black paper and white chalk. The teacher circulated while this art was done to assist the Dogs in making the most accurate copies possible. The resulting artwork occupied another wall in my classroom: row after row of identical white chalk snowmen on black paper differing only by the name of the child artist at the bottom.

The Turtles were given the same assignment as the Dogs but the art teacher didn't expect much of them and just patrolled to keep order. Many of their pieces of black paper became thrown airplanes while many pieces of chalk became missiles to shoot them down. The wall in my classroom set aside for the Turtles had a variety of crumbled pieces of black paper with varying chalk scribbles; few looked much like snowmen. The teacher was accepting of this for the Turtles as she assumed their abilities were limited, eschewing a "one size fits all" mainstream approach to teaching art.

She was of course badly mistaken. We knew by the 1960s that IQ scores assessed a very narrow range of ability and were often biased. We knew by then that IQ test scores were not independent of education but rather reflected its quality. I had been fortunate to work with Robert L. Green and colleagues on testing the thousands of children displaced from Virginia schools for four years to avoid desegregation: intelligence and its measures clearly depended on schooling.

We shared this perspective with our friendly art teacher but she was not convinced. She pointed out that these three groups were treated differently in *all* their subject areas by the teachers and did not feel it was her place to make policy changes. She shared that her Principal was very firm about this.

The graduate students and I made a private prediction. This was the only public school in a very small rural university town. It seemed to us that these children were being socialized for community roles as adults. The Eagles were trained to think for themselves and would become adaptive business or professional leaders. The Dogs were being trained to conform and follow orders exactly and would become the uninspiring but reliable employees of the Eagles. The Turtles were being trained to fail and would become the clients of the various community institutions serving misfits, including the jail. We predicted that as adults they will fill the roles the school had prepared them for.

Twenty-five years later I participated in an international psychology congress in Halifax, Nova Scotia, and took some travel time to revisit this rural university town. Many of my former graduate students still lived there. Sadly, our predictions for the Eagles, Dogs, and Turtles had come true.

How about educating *all* our children as the Eagles were? Don't they deserve to fly as high as they can? That is both a global opportunity and an uncompleted responsibility.

Inner Wisdom and
Roberto Moulon

Theme: *Magic Man* Heart

In 1966, Roberto Moulon was the psychiatrist in charge of Hawaii's hospitalized Neighbor Island patients.

His family ethnicity was French Guatemalan Indian. He looked somewhat like a tanned and older Herve Villechaize from the TV show *Fantasy Island*. Deeper voice.

I was a psychologist working with Hawaii State Hospital's Metropolitan Honolulu patients. My psychologist colleagues were following an Existentialist practice, which was great.

But Moulon had a Freudian perspective and that was worth a listen as well. Plus tales of his past private practice. A sample?

Inner Wisdom

Dr. Moulon told me about a new patient in his past private practice.

A large anxious man inhabited his couch while Roberto sat behind the young man's view in Freudian traditional pose, casually lighting his pipe.

The patient rambled on for some time but finally got to the fear that had brought him to this psychiatrist. He said he had been unable to have an erection during a sexual opportunity with a woman he had met in Rome. He wondered if this meant he was damaged or getting old before his time.

Moulon, in a quiet but authoritative French accent from behind the patient, told him to say more about the specific event.

With this invitation, the young man went on: *"We were somewhat drunk but still able to walk. The night was beautiful. People were everywhere enjoying their time together. We came to a huge fountain by the Vatican. Reminded me of the movie La Dolce Vita."*

The Trevi Fountain, Rome.

He continued:

"In that very moment it WAS a sweet life for us! We were spontaneous. Ignoring the other people around us, we

stripped off our clothes and jumped into the water around the fountain. Let the water fall over us. We kissed. She pressed against me. I have always risen to such occasions. But not this time. My penis refused to rise. Doctor PLEASE! Tell me what this means!"

Moulon was silent for a moment while he puffed on his pipe.

Finally his authoritative voice intoned:

"The meaning? Well of course. Clearly your penis has more sense than you do."

Not the Trevi Fountain, Rome. They love water too though.

The Psychiatrists

At our hospital, psychiatrists fell into two categories.

To begin with, all had been trained as medical doctors before moving into the psychiatric specialty. Some became outstanding physicians.

But most in that training, usually a residency, never had any supervised experience doing psychotherapy.

Instead they learned the biomedical tools of prescribing psychiatric medications, the sadly destructive electroconvulsive treatment (ECT), and, in those days, even lobotomies (still recommended by our administrator). These methods were at best unhelpful and at worst destructive, occasionally lethal.

This left most psychiatrists in this category at a loss to be effective with the hospital patients.

Further, some were all but hopeless at working anywhere else.

An immigrant physician from Turkey comes to mind as an example. He spoke no English at all so he could not understand any of his patients or staff. Diverse as Hawaii was, nobody on hospital staff knew Turkish to be his translator. He lasted in his job for quite a few months though.

In category two, on the other hand, a few of the other physicians had excellent psychotherapy training. Of these Roberto Moulon was the most experienced and probably the most *akamai* or wisest of his psychiatrist peers.

The state of Hawaii released an employee sick leave study for the previous calendar year, broken down for our hospital by discipline.

The psychologists and social workers had taken *zero* days of sick leave in that time. We pretty much never felt we could miss a workday, given the substantial need in our wards.

The nurses and psychiatrists had taken the most sick leave days, higher than the state employee average for their discipline. In addition, they both had the largest turnovers. Other studies identified psychiatry as having issues with suicides and drug addiction.

We understood the nursing statistics. As a group, they earned the least of any hospital disciplines while expected to do the most work, often with long extra hours. Compared to their psychiatrist supervisors, they did more for less. Much more for much less.

The nurses also fell into two categories. The beginning nurses were usually highly motivated to learn, dedicated to their patients, and expected success in their chosen career. They knew they had a challenging job. Certainly they could have gone into a less stressful nursing environment. For them it was a career they cared about. They were also very decent people. Over the years, a few of them survived to be highly effective long term senior nurses.

But others burned out or became cynical, expecting little success at work and less reward for their effort. No wonder their absence total and turnover were high.

The psychiatrists without the training they needed to do their job well were naturally stressed and it showed in the statistics.

Worse, they were the ones chosen to lead the hospital supervision and administration, again requiring people skills few of them had available. They could feel frustrated, stressed, unappreciated.

Even when by some luck they did manage success at the magic they felt was required of them, anticipated staff or patient applause was lacking.

'WHAT DO YOU MEAN 'IT'S A BIT MUDDY'?'

Of course, many were only there to qualify for licensing to do private practice and would leave as soon as they had acquired the needed hours.

Some though, lacking the talent they needed, still gave it their best. This could lead to legend. Here are two examples:

(1) Love in Hawaii

A psychiatrist claimed to cure locked ward patients at the state hospital from a distance.

He sits in his office with their files, never meeting them, and practices existential extremism: he assumes their traumatic pathology stems from him, apologizes, and wishes them love.

He reports that his patients get better while the rest get worse. This got a lot of play in the media.

Well, if this marvelous effect can be validated, it could mean more than a psychiatrist finding ways to avoid patients and collect a paycheck, interesting in its own right.

It would assume a certain existential narcissism: he is the cause and cure of the trauma of others.

Of course, it might also be that the normal treatment of psychiatric patients in a locked ward is iatrogenic and that by withholding treatment (no ECT or psychiatric drugs or interpersonal intervention) and staying in his office he is demonstrating placebo power, moral treatment, or just leaving people alone.

On the other hand, if all the current problems of our human community truly come from him, he needs to start apologizing and sending global love without delay.

(2) Dining on Air

Another psychiatrist at Hawaii State Hospital, before my time there, completed a legendary experiment.

He had tried fasting, vegan diets, and other cultural paths to enlightenment. By reaching a higher plain of his own existence, he had confidence he could be more effective with his patients.

Since, by general staff observation, he lacked the knowledge or experience to benefit any of his patients. Though despite this, all agreed he had the will to do so.

The gap between psychiatric training and successful treatment fit was a common stress for hospital physicians with a conscience. This man was one such.

And so it was that they tried not to be appalled when one Monday morning the psychiatrist announced that he had not eaten or had anything to drink all weekend.

The one exception, he had read of and practiced nourishment only from the air itself. He was now a Breatharian.

While those practicing this technique still imbibe liquids, their psychiatrist followed the strictest path he had found, one in search of the best outcome, quickly. He would dine only on air and sunlight.

His nursing staff was dubious but also relieved he was doing this first on himself before prescribing it for his patients. Or worse, for them.

The psychiatrist managed almost a full day of work before he was carried out on a stretcher. He was said to have survived but never returned to his hospital job.

The staff wondered who or what would take his place next.

Note: I am reminded of my profoundly underfunded program's weekly report to the full faculty of a for-profit university, with most of the tuition going to the owning corporation.

I told them of the farmer who had run short of feed for his horse and fed the animal only the half ration left. To the farmer's surprise, the horse adjusted to this meager meal in a few days and worked as before. The joyful farmer called a meeting to share his finding with all the other farmers. In preparation he cut the horse's rations in half again. It took longer for the horse to adjust but that he did. When the meeting finally convened, the horse's owner shared this opportunity to save on feed with enthusiasm, despite the ending of his talk when he breathlessly announced that only days before he had cut his horse's daily ration to zero. Just when he was ready to announce his success to all of them, he had some bad fortune. The horse had unexpectedly died.

Following this unusual report of my own, the top administrator present stood and said *"Dr. Morgan, please elevate that sad story you just told us with at least something more positive!"*

I did my best: *"Here in my program we like to think of our resources as like a glass 5% full."*

Candid honesty means always having your bags packed.

Tom Thumb

A brilliant colleague from those days, Albuquerque psychologist Joe Alexander, emailed me a reminder of his experience with Dr. Moulon: *"Roberto was our moderator for our afternoon monthly case review. Psychiatrists, Psychologists, interested Social Workers (only LaVey Lau actually) took turns presenting clinical cases. Then Roberto would make observations. We took turns presenting and taking minutes. Sometimes the psychiatric residents and psychology interns were invited. My favorite session was a presentation by Moulon called 'Seven Sick and Sinful Sisters'. "*

Yes. Comparing Roberto to most of the other psychiatrists was a low bar. Moulon was really great at his work. Or calling.

I didn't get to hear Joe's favorite *"Seven Sick and Sinful Sisters"* but I can share my most memorable case conference with Roberto. About a deadly Tom Thumb.

The headlines were remarkably bad and all over the state. A chronic mental patient, recently returned to her family on a conditional discharge, had murdered all five of her children, including a baby.

She was eventually sent to the care of a locked hospital ward run by Dr. Moulon.

Nobody on his staff wanted anything to do with this patient. All refused to treat her.

Hawaii in that era put children above all other priorities, probably still does. A killer of children, especially her own, was the worst human being they could imagine. Especially her own. Hate for any patient was rare in this professional group. This one they hated.

Moulon had a staff rebellion on his hands.

He called a case conference meeting for the very next morning. Invited me to join him there. Which in Hawaii was at 7 AM (so the day could end early enough for daylight swimming and surfing). I avoid mornings but in this case I definitely agreed. I thought Roberto would need some support.

He did not.

Once assembled around the conference table, we all turned to Moulon at its head. He sat there elevated on his chair, and quietly asked for a brief status report on the new patient. A nurse complied.

The patient was heavily sedated and slept in a locked room. In her waking moments she denied doing anything wrong, asked about her children, dropped back to sleep. Her body functions and diet were normal. She was more than in denial. She was delusional, psychotic. No adequate reality contact. Hopeless.

Then a social worker briefly reiterated what everybody in the state already knew. The patient had been in and out of the state hospital for years. In each of five of her exits she had become pregnant. Her children, including the baby, had been in foster care but had been reassembled to be with her for this last discharge. The hospital administrator, a psychiatrist, had personally approved this arrangement, saying that children belonged with their mother. The administrator was now providing no comment other than saying it was in Dr. Moulon's hands.

(We all knew that the administrator had also released another patient as cured who subsequently climbed a tower and shot people to death. The administrator, affirming her decision that the now deceased killer was mentally healthy at discharge, had blamed it on an overseen minor brain tumor found in the autopsy. Though medical research has yet to find a part of the brain capable of directing somebody to climb a tower and shoot people. Now, with this new patient, she was fully hands off. It was Moulon's headache.)

When all the reports were done, tensely and tersely, Roberto let them settle for a minute. Until finally we had all turned to him for comment, direction. Tense crowd.

Finally he calmly said *"I will tell you a story. You may not understand it. I will have no interruptions. When I am done, we may discuss the relevance."* He continued.

The calm voice with the French accent from this brilliant man in that early morning seemed unworldly. Especially as he began. But we all listened.

"You surely recall the story of little Tom Thumb. He and his brothers, also little, had left home and were far from anywhere they knew. Why they left home did not matter at the time because it was getting dark

and they were hungry. Wait! They smelled some delicious food. It was coming from a very big cabin on a hill. Quickly Tom led them to the cabin door, much taller than they had ever seen, and Tom knocked on it hard with his walking stick.

The door soon opened and a giant woman looked down at them.

Tom asked if they could come in. The night was dark now and they were hungry.

The giant considered, smiled, and invited them in, just in time for supper.

Tom and his brothers sat down at a huge table. There already were the giant's children. They were the same in number as those with Tom although, being giant's children, they must have been much younger since they were all about the same height as Tom. The giant mother sat at one end of the table and the giant father at the other. The food already prepared was delicious and everybody ate until full, maybe a little more than that.

The giant mother promised an even better breakfast and then led all the children to a bedroom so they could sleep after such a meal. She left them alone and shut the door.

The bedroom needed no beds as the floor was as soft as a fine mattress. The giant's children had seemed shy to Tom at first but even now they spoke not at all to their guests. Soon all were asleep, the giant woman's children on one side while Tom and his brothers soon were asleep on the other.

Tom woke in the middle of the night. Maybe he first just wanted to answer a call of nature. He opened the bedroom door and could hear some noise from the kitchen. Looking for directions, he walked to the kitchen door. Here stood the giant mother talking to her giant husband who was seated at the table, back to Tom. The mother was sharpening a huge knife and a massive pot of boiling water was over the fire.

Tom heard her say to her husband "Almost time to slice off their heads and pop them in the pot. They'll be a great stew for breakfast."

The giant husband said "Now? But it's dark in there. No moon tonight. How will you know which ones to slice?"

His wife said "All our guests have goofy stocking hats and they went to bed with them on. Our children don't sleep with any hats. Could do it with my eyes shut."

"You'll have to. Its pitch dark in there."

At this, Tom ran back to the bedroom, He took off his hat and the hats of his brothers, putting each one on the head of one of the giant's children. His eyes were adapted to the crack of light coming through the bedroom door from the kitchen. Then he very quietly woke his brothers, shushed them, and all slipped out of the cabin. Just as they left, Tom looked back through a window and saw the giant mother with her huge knife and a massive bag enter the bedroom. Breakfast will be a surprise for sure.

Then Tom and his hatless brothers ran until they were safe."

Moulon stopped there. Paused. Then: *"As to our new patient. What do you think she thought she was doing when she killed her own children?"*

And then he told us.

Moulon had been working with the patient herself during her lucid moments. At first she denied everything, even insisting they were all alive and fine. She said it was all a misunderstanding. She had just killed mice on her lawn, not people. Mice? Maybe roaches or rats? Not clear she said.

A neighbor had reported to police that the patient had just backed her car out of the driveway on a sunny afternoon. Her children were playing on the lawn near the driveway. Except for the baby who had crawled under a rear tire. The neighbor saw the woman driver get out of the car to see what all the yelling was about. Then she saw what was left of the baby after the car tire had crushed it. The children on the lawn were crying and screaming. The neighbor went home and called the police. When the police got there, all the children had been killed and their mother was unconscious. Comatose. Overwhelmed.

Killing her baby was a genuine accident. The rest were a hopeless delusional exit from an impossible situation. She was the giant mother who had killed her own children without meaning to. Tom Thumb was fictitious. Her overwhelming tragedy was not. The dead children could no longer be helped. If she could be helped, even a little, we should try.

Moulon said he would assign himself to continue treatment. Then he assigned all of us to either be kind with any contact or to avoid all contact if we had no kindness in us.

We filed away quietly. The rebellion was over. Sadness not.

Over the next few weeks Moulon called on every bit of his brilliance to build a relationship with this lost woman. He made progress. She was his primary client. Not us. Not the administrator. Not the press. Not the public. He did his best and it helped.

He warned me that her delusion was clearly a functional protection against acknowledging the horror of her murder of her own children. When she lifts that delusional protection, she becomes vulnerable. That would be the most dangerous time for her. He planned to guide her through it.

On a Friday he told me, elated, she had dropped her delusion. She was heavily sedated again. Moulon prepared for the key therapy on the following Monday.

We wondered together what in life could a person do, coming to grips with what she had done. Maybe spend the rest of her life volunteering at the Kalaupappa Leper Colony? Study law in a cell? Develop spirituality? Clearly it would be her choice and only after some serious incarceration could she make it. That was Friday.

On Sundays a minister, claiming to be the patient's minister, had visited. He was not her minister. In fact she had no such person in her life. This "minister" was there to get her to admit her crime. On that last Sunday visit she did so. He told her she would roast in hell and everybody would always hate her. She didn't deserve to live! Not the therapy Moulon had planned.

The staff escorted the fake minister out when they heard him yelling these things at the patient.

That night they found she had hung herself in her locked room.

Monday morning was possibly Moulon's worst day. Not great for any of us, but especially crushing for Roberto. What to do with such grief?

We took on the next case. One we both had patients involved in. And we learned something new.

Sibling Bondage: A Parricide and his Brother

Roberto Moulon and I coined the term "sibling bondage" as a pathological opposite to the better known and frequently manifested "sibling rivalry".

An example follows from my 2012 *"Trauma Psychology in Context"* book.

The Discovery of Sibling Bondage: A Parricide & his Brother

The second Manuel killed his father, he was able to love him again. But now his anger was satisfied, he had a larger problem. Putting down the shotgun, he called the police and said "I kill my father. Come get me." Then he said nothing more: not when they came, not in jail, and not when he was carried off the plane frozen to his chair en route to Hawaii State Hospital. He took up residence in his catatonic state and remained in apparent safety there for the duration.

Only days after his arrival, his younger brother Anthony was also flown in for hospitalization.

Anthony was the youngest, a stocky teenager, and, far from catatonic, was swearing vengeance to his father's ghost, or so he said. Mother, the sole survivor in the family home, had decided Anthony needed to be flown to Oahu to be with his brother and away from her. She was considered to be mentally disabled, but she wasn't stupid. Speaking to invisible beings, after Manuel's action, just didn't seem right.

Anthony was assigned to my Young Adult Day Program while Manuel was taken under the care of Dr. Roberto Moulun, a psychoanalyst formerly of the Menninger Clinic, who began coordinating the treatment of the brothers with me. This was not always easy.

Anthony was quite friendly and rational with two exceptions. The first was whenever he saw Dr. Moulon, who resembled his deceased father. At this time, he would bellow and chase the psychiatrist into his office. Moulun found it difficult to relate effectively with Anthony from the safe side of his locked office door.

The second stressor was the monthly visit of his mother. On viewing her, Anthony would punch the air and loudly swear vengeance for his dead father. Soon Mother was only visiting Manuel, even though these visits were somewhat unusual: Manuel sat frozen in his chair where he had been carried outside to the front grass and sunshine. For hours Mother would sit quietly next to him along with some local relatives. Not a word was ever said beyond "Hello Manuel" *and* "Goodbye Manuel".

Moulon and I sifted through the family history. Manuel and Anthony were the youngest of a large Portuguese family on a small rural island. Their mother was barely functional, her great achievement being the household cooking and cleaning. Her husband was an absolute tyrant, completely controlling all under his roof with regular beatings. He alone would go into town and shop. His children were discouraged from going to school and were not allowed to speak unless spoken to first by him. The expression 'poor communication' does little justice to the managed silences under this father's regime. The children left home as soon as they could: boys joined the army while girls got pregnant and married. Eventually only Manuel and Anthony remained.

Of these, Manuel was his father's favorite. They worked together in the fields in rare and quiet harmony. Anthony, at 15 the youngest, was another story. Although he was as large as Manuel, he had a heart murmur. Mother kept him close. So close in fact, he slept with her right up to the day he was hospitalized. Father wanted Anthony to work in the fields with his brother but, apparently for the first time in their marriage, she refused, saying she would leave if Anthony had to do such work. The Patriarch possibly did not see himself doing cooking or cleaning. He gave in.

Anthony went to public school and did reasonably well. This favoritism was not missed by Manuel. One day Manuel himself ordered his brother to come out to the fields and work. Anthony declined and their parents supported him. The next day Manuel went into town to enlist in the Army. Unfortunately for him, the recruiters were now required to give an intelligence test which he failed, nor did it occur to him to apply for officer training instead.

Manuel returned home in a foul mood. He once again worked with his father in the fields but began muttering that his father was a communist and a "revisionist", words heard on the family radio. It may well be that taking Anthony's side was a revisionist thing for his father to do, given Manuel's former status as his father's favored child. The father did not know what a revisionist was but he knew that a 'communist' was supposed to be something very bad. He finally beat Manuel until he fell into the fields, covered with blood and bruises. That night Manuel borrowed his father's shotgun and killed him in his sleep.

As time went by, Moulon's work with Manuel paid off. Manuel began moving again and in a few weeks he was one of the happiest residents in the hospital. He worked hard at his 'industrial therapy' (which meant hospital garbage collection) and developed a close bond with Doctor Moulon, his therapist and father figure. ("But I'll never take him on a hunting trip" said Moulon.).

Anthony for his part thrived in my Young Adult Program. Despite his harsh background, he was of normal intelligence and made many new friends. Oh he still chased Roberto Moulon into his office (but now smiled when he did so) and became quietly anxious when Mother visited. But that was all. He also spent time with his brother and often left him gifts. Asked about Anthony, Manuel would smile and say "My brother loves me now." Asked about Manuel, Anthony would say "He killed him for me."

Why had Anthony been so belligerent at home, hallucinating a dead parent?

Moulon believed it was guilt for wishing his father dead. This may be but certainly there was trauma involved. Eventually, Anthony explained it to me. He believed in an afterlife in which his father's malevolent ghost was still around. Only this ghost was worse than his father had been before: Father was now invisible and with ghostly powers, Father could tell that Anthony wanted him dead more than Manuel did. Father would hurt him if he didn't swear vengeance and be convincing. On the plus side, Anthony believed that his father's ghost could only be found in his old house or by his mother's side. So he enjoyed his new life on Oahu without trauma.

And why chase Dr. Moulon?

"At first I didn't like the way he looked."

"Like your Father?"

"Yes."

"Now you know he's not your father."

"Oh yes. But now I like the way he runs."

And Anthony smiled.

The children of loving and competent parents normally experience a rivalry for parental affection. This "sibling rivalry" is quite normal. On the other hand, children of abusive or non-competent parents may band together against the common enemy but this is a relationship based on trauma and danger. As such, it can be handicapping or even violently destructive. Moulon and I decided to call this "sibling bondage".

If our perspective was correct, then the older siblings would soon also be in distress. Checking with the local clinic on the Mother's island, within weeks of the death of their father, every one of the brothers and sisters had been in for treatment. The eldest daughter had recurring nightmares of an open coffin in her living room into which she dared not look. Under Moulon's consultation, all received therapist encouragement to accept their anger and its Shadow, a death wish for their Father, as a normal traumatic reaction to his brutality, and to face his memory without guilt or fear. Today, I would add forgiveness as well, but in this instance Moulon's directions were effective. Shadows lose their power when a light is shined on them. All the brothers and sisters recovered. A community can also be led into sibling bondage, transformed by trauma, members bound together into a closed system by hatred. This bond is also pathological and needs healing.

* * *

That was then. How about now? In looking at our contemporary world, we can see sibling bondage play out on a much broader political and social stage. Cultish domestic terrorism is such an extreme. Or even the lesser taking of horse de-wormer while shunning life-saving vaccines.

Which body part should be credited with more sense?

What would Dr. Moulon say if he were here to observe?

We sure miss him.

Mighty Mose

Themes: *Juliet of the Spirits theme* Nino Rota; *I Ain't Got Nothing but the Blues* Mose Allison

Wheels

My father was 35 before he could afford his first car and so was I. This meant I walked everywhere. Distances too large or time sensitive for pedestrian travel, I used public transport- buses, trains, cabs, planes. This had several benefits. Not having a car with payments, fuel, repairs, licenses, insurance, was financially like having one less child to support (my parenting responsibility had been zero to five). Being a single parent, this mattered. Another benefit was great health by regular outdoor exercise. The main drawback was that I had never learned to drive.

I did take a Driver Ed class in high school. Got perfect scores on the written exam. Then the final test behind the wheel of a 1950s stick shift challenge. In the car with me were my driving teacher and another student named Lenny LaCongo. Lenny went first and drove relaxed as though he had been born to it. My turn. So foot on clutch, brake, accelerator, manage gear shifts, watch traffic- all at once. Well, no accidents but this was multi-tasking beyond my newcomer ability. I was no Lenny LaCongo. I didn't pass. Did learn that I wasn't ready to drive a stick shift. Waited patiently for decades until automatic was the norm. Much less self-driving cars in the 21st century.

I did recently look up Lenny online. Owns a used car chain.

Of course, they don't call these used cars "*used*" anymore. Now they are "*certified pre-owned*". Occurs to me that the term *certified pre-owned* might well be already in use ironically on dating apps for previously disappointed hopefuls of all genders with a sense of humor. If the prior match was really unfortunate, the term "*used*" might best come back to be applied online with more emotional accuracy. Seeing yourself as having been used or pre-owned is no fun. Until you can eventually make fun of it.

Plus from here on: Stay free.

Peace Corps, Molokai, Hawaii

1960s.

To become a Peace Corps Volunteer required a three month training in a similar site to their destination of a western Pacific Island before these Peace Corps Trainees (PCTs) could call themselves a Peace Corps Volunteer (PCVs). Not everybody made it through this training to get to their two-Year adventure.

I had a full time job in the psychology department at the Hawaii State Hospital on Oahu. It included seeing patients in the metropolitan Honolulu region, while developing and running a day program for all 30 children who were resident hospital patients. I was also involved in ML King's projects plus government consultations for Head Start, desegregation grants, etc. Plus a family of five at home. So I was busy. Even at my middle twenties, this was a lot to multi-task. Kind of like trying to drive a stick shift.

So when the psychologists in my department took on being field assessment officers for the three month Peace Corps training project on Molokai, I didn't see how I could fit that in too.

We did get two graduate psychology students from the University of Hawaii to share the work: Mike Compton and Len Elkind. And psychologist John Exner was leading our assessment group as Field Selection Officer. Just finishing his classic book on Rorschach.

So I signed up for one Thursday a week. Fly from Honolulu to Molokai Wednesday night and fly back Thursday night. In that concentrated day I divided my 30 trainees, headed if successful to the island of Ponape, into three groups, ten each, meeting 90 minutes per group. Then individual meeting as needed with trainees, peers, training staff, Exner, and either of the two psychiatrists being rented for the training.

Waiting for me at the airport was a rental car with keys, ready for me to drive to the training site. I had told the Peace Corps staffer that I had no driver's license. He said in Molokai it didn't matter. I said I had no driving experience. He said turn the keys in the ignition and take the straight road across the island to the site. No Problem.

I looked at this little stick shift car and invoked hope for both of us. Got in and drove.

It was a straight shot on the highway. Uneventful except for the construction to the side at the halfway point. The car did hit an orange cone as I sped by and, as it shot up into the atmosphere, my rearview mirror framed some fist waving construction crew.

I never took the gear out of first but got to the site safely after all. Began to feel less anxious. Not hard to drive then.

Did my day. Fulfilling. Great people all around. They liked the *Bogardus Social Distance* test I had adapted for use with my groups, as did Exner.

Time to drive to the house Peace Corps was providing us. Food, sleep soon, drive to the airport in the morning. Thought I finally had the driving thing under control.

A local woman was leasing this home to Peace Corps. Very welcoming. I was sharing it on Thursday night with my assessment partners Compton and Elkind.

Len Elkind had a young Basset Hound canine companion named Mose. Mike Compton liked Mose and other dogs but he had strong feelings that Mose was not to be allowed in the rented house. Len complied. Mose was chained to a pillar inside the garage. Water and food dish within reach. Regular walks with Len for exercise and evacuation.

It was a strong chain that kept Mose tied to that central pillar. He could not have been awfully happy about any of this. Yet he had a trustingly lethargic approach to his situation. Which likely he considered temporary like everything else in his changing life.

No barking, whining, growling, biting. Everybody liked Mose. He made the best of everything, more than could have been said about the rest of us today.

So that first night I was driving to this Molokai home. Still anxious but losing a few pounds for that wouldn't be missed and amplified the appetite for supper. So, finding some confidence, I managed to get all the way into third gear while still keeping the car on the road. As I approached the house, I declined to gear down. It had been hard enough to get there. I just took my foot off the accelerator and readied it on the brake, I spun at speed into a right turn to the driveway. Made it. Lined right up. My foot was already softly caressing the brake and then slammed it down.

Going right toward the garage at the end of the driveway. The car seemed to consider stopping for a second but then it did.

Just after we crashed through the garage door, heading right toward Mose.

A few feet from his former location, I got out of the stopped car and looked to Mose.

He wasn't there. Only the broken chain remained.

Looking out the place where the door had been, I could see Mose in the distance, shooting like a bullet over a hill down the street. One could see the vestige of a broken steel chain dragging behind him.

What a powerful hound! Free of his chains by a mighty effort. Maybe an event I could have had something to do with.

Sure, I paid for the repairs. And yes, Peace Corps had me picked up and dropped off at the airport after that.

Most of my trainees completed their three months successfully and on to Ponape to contribute their years of service.

Peace Corps in later years reduced the three month training to three days or did it in the actual destination.

Next

I learned to drive a decade later in Colorado.

Compton and Elkind completed their doctorate and had brilliant careers as psychologists. We're still great friends.

Mose went on to other adventures after leaving Molokai.

In the end he ran free in the huge contained area of a wealthy human. Free of cars or chains.

His powerful escape remains etched in our memory.

And in the archives of the Puppy Union.

A Gweiloh in Hong Kong

Theme: *Enter the Dragon* Lalo Schifrin

1967. My post-doc clinical psychology internship in Hawaii was done.

My new wife with her own three not-so-new-to-her children, were all safe and happy on Oahu.

Time for me to explore our next stop. I flew to Hong Kong.

I rented an apartment for a month. It came with an Amah, a live-in person (with her own living space there) to maintain the home and, to a very limited extent, me as well.

She spoke no English but was perceptive of gestures and body language plus, at times, she called in a bilingual friend from another apartment for translation.

The English language newspapers headlined a riot going on in which acid was thrown intto the faces of Hong Kong Chinese police.

A massive response from them was suppressed reasonably by the British government so as to avoid expanding the carnage. Even so, some police had killed some acid throwers.

Now this burning weapon and more spread to people on all sides along with passersby on nobody's side. Something to consider.

That first day I avoided the acid tossing area and made my way to the three banks.

I took a rickshaw since I still hadn't learned the walking routes. A man who said he was 86 years old was pulling it. Lean wiry muscles with not much effort.

While I admired his strength and stamina, at 26 I felt embarrassed to be transported by a man sixty years my senior. Too colonial, exploitive for me. But this *was* a British colony at the time.

On arrival I tipped him at the level I would a taxi driver in Hawaii. He said it was too much, a month's salary. But I knew the custom.

He declined to accept it three times but when I said no, he should keep it, the third time he accepted and made the money disappear. He smiled, nodded, and he too disappeared fast before I might change my mind. Three times was the charm.

Time to open an account.

My first stop, naturally, was my own country's bank. The Bank of America. No snobs expected there.

Nope. But in front of the bank stood a marine guard. His rifle at the ready, complete with bayonet.

I asked him what the problem was, expecting to hear about acid throwers. He asked if I was an American. Yes, I was. He told me I could come in then. Said he was there to protect white Americans like me from the Chinese.

No thanks. I moved on.

To the British bank. No bayonet guard in front. Inside it was clean and impressive.

The clerk asked me if I had an account.

No, I was there to open one. Had the money I had arrived with, ready to deposit. He said I would need two written references from two current bank customers to open an account. I said I just had come to Hong Kong and didn't know any of their customers yet.

Conserving words, he just nodded toward the entrance, meaning *"there's the door- walk out now through it"*. Or, per the Southern USA phrase that occurred to me. *"Don't let the door hit you where the good Lord split you"*.

And my felt response *"Bless his tiny little heart."*

I wasn't sure he would understand my finger gesture that followed but, in case he did, I exited as requested. I wouldn't be back.

That left the Chinese bank. Okay then.

They were very friendly. Spoke English fluently. Brought in the person in charge. Who explained to me that China had no diplomatic relations with my home country. Therefore they were not allowed to open a new account for me. That diplomatic relationship would come five years later in 1972 with Nixon:

Too late for me back in 1967.

But the Chinese banker had given me a card with an address on it. A smaller anonymous currency exchange that foreigners used. They took my money and opened an account. No, I'm not sure what nationality they were even today. European? They didn't say. But they were honest, foreigners aplenty used them, and I had no regrets.

They also printed out business cards for me, necessary for any professional work. Or anything else. Hello in business there and then always meant an exchange of business cards. Name, title, business, and contact information. English on one side, Chinese on the other.

Reveled in the music, art, colors, parades, laughter. Food. I did love being there.

I was now ready to open a practice in Clinical Psychology.

There were none then.

Looking in newspapers, directories, inquiries with medical individuals, everywhere and anywhere, the same conclusion. Not yet, not there.

I did find a newspaper ad for psychotherapy services from somebody who proudly proclaimed that he had completed a psychology class at the University of South Africa.

Well, talk about an opportunity to get in from the ground floor. Being first is an event that never gets overtaken. The need was great. A chance to build the discipline from scratch within that vibrant culture. *With* that vibrant culture.

Still, the daily English language newspaper headlined more tourist deaths from the growing unrest. Should I bring my young family into the midst of this colonial struggle? Would they be safe? *Acid?* Would we be on the wrong side?

But now I had this new family. They either come now to join me or I return to join them.

I called this family long distance for a consultation.

If I were a bachelor on my own, I would definitely stay, follow this path. Considering their own safety, they deserved a say, a veto if they chose.

I asked them to take a chance and join me.

No contest. Unanimous at their end. No! Come home! As they like to say, often, in the 50ᵗʰ state: *"Lucky be in Hawaii"*.

I still had a month left on my apartment lease.

With the help of the downstairs translator I explained that I would be going back to rejoin my family in Hawaii very soon. But I would pay her the full salary for the coming month now plus some more in consideration of my departure.

She took this well so, through the translator, I invited her to a farewell dinner that night at the best restaurant she knew of. She conferred with the translator in animated Chinese, smiling, excited.

The translator said to me that her recommendation for the top restaurant in Hong Kong had been accepted by the Amah. Further, she explained that this was likely to be a once-in-a-lifetime experience for the Amah who, surely I had noticed, ate only one meal a day from a very healthy large bowl of foul-smelling gruel. Of course she had no clothes suitable for this occasion. Yet, for a small stipend, very small considering, the translator would take her to a store to purchase said apparel. Agreed.

Before our dinner, I packed for the return, bought those gifts that my Hawaii family saw as the primary reason for my stay in Hong Kong, and dressed my best for the evening event.

Our translator had booked a central table in a very elegant restaurant. My Amah matched this elegance though she communicated through clear gestures that this was all just a beautiful dream for her.

The patrons, all seemingly successful Hong Kong Chinese of an age, were apparently wealthy or famous enough to match the setting. I recognized some that were celebrities.

The food arrived in colorful waves, as regular as ocean tides. Small portions, each better than the last. Teacups were never allowed to be empty, avoiding any sign of wait staff inhospitality. A few dishes had an egg on top, later explained to me that the chef was choosing to do this as a habit from post-World War Two egg shortages, making its superlative use an elegance.

I had a great appetite then and managed it all. Though my Amah, a slight diminutive woman, outdid me by far. During her one restroom trip, the waiter refolded her napkin, whisked any crumbs off the table, and introduced himself. He was Luis, Chinese-Portuguese from Macao.

When my Amah returned, Luis stepped away, and we completed a variety of desserts. Since we had all arrived as an elite cohort at a scheduled time, all tables were more or less served simultaneously. So we all completed our dining fairly close together. A musical note from somewhere signaled this end.

At that point everybody but me, yes including my Amah, belched very loudly. At every table. The wait staff seemed pleased. As for me, it was the only time I felt alone on an alien planet. I love swimming in new cultures. But this Monty Python moment was a puzzlement.

Luis rushed to my side. *"Not like the dinner?"* he asked with great concern. I asked about the communal belching. Relieved, he explained it was a way the Chinese diners expressed appreciation for fine food and service, second only to an expected generous gratuity. Oh.

Again, too early by a few years for Nixon to be in such a setting but when I saw another photo of that eventually, it reminded me of our dinner. I can only imagine how he might have reacted if his

Beijing hosts showed similar appreciation. (He's already holding his chopsticks in an insultingly incorrect manner.)

As I paid the bill, with an American way too generous gratuity, Luis warmed up even more, my new best friend. Since all diners were still at close by tables, he leaned over to confide his Chinese name to me. These are given at birth and remain family secrets thereafter.

He asked me if I had a Chinese name as well. A polite request since that was not expected from an American visitor. I surprised him.

"Yes, I do have a Chinese name" I replied, loud enough to be heard from all tables.

Luis apologized for asking, no longer whispering.

But I relieved him of worry.

"No problem. I was given it here in Hong Kong. Everybody seems to refer to me in this way. My Chinese name is … GWEILO!"

This translates to the racial epithet *'Ghostly White One"* or *'Foreign Devil'*, as I knew.

All the patrons laughed even louder than they had belched, including Luis.

Laughter: an American alternative to a cohort's appreciative belching chorus.

My Amah at first was blushing, embarrassed, but soon laughed with the rest.

Smiled at me all the way home.

Glowing from her Cinderella evening.

The Morgan House Ghost

Themes: *Ghost Riders* Johnny Cash/Willie Nelson;

This happened in 1969 in western Nova Scotia. Near the end of the next 1970s decade I shared it with Robert Monroe and his daughter at their second OBE training session in Virginia. Elisabeth Kubler Ross stayed past the first session to hear it.

Tony Harvester

Tony Harvester would still want to be headlined here. Done.

I bought a racehorse for twenty Canadian dollars.

He had been named Tony Harvester though likely he never knew or cared about that. Tony was about to be "put down" or killed. He was a year past the age where the other horses stopped racing. Worse, he had pulled up lame in one leg, limping painfully to the stables.

Still he was the most social animal the human handlers had ever known. Tony loved horses, dogs, and even humans.

His positive attitude so endeared him to the humans that they were glad to let him live if they could sell him to me for only twenty dollars.

True though, Tony had never won a race.

He always ran with the fastest horse, loving to run with a companion, but the fastest horse wanted to win and Tony, ever the great friend, always let them come in first. If there were several horses all pushing to win, he would pace them and then allow them to *all* cross the finish line first. No abuse from a jockey changed his mind.

So the horses liked him too. Exactly the world he most enjoyed living in. Especially that one last race where he realized he loved racing. And won easily. Better than possible.

Now the real cost of owning a racehorse includes more than the purchase price. You need food, vet care, grooming, exercise, and a comfortable place to keep him.

The last at least I already had waiting.

Morgan House

Martin Luther King Jr. was assassinated in 1968. He was not yet even 40. I was not yet 30. Our years with him were over and his killers were in power. Fed up, my family began anew the next year in the country to the north.

Specifically I began a job at a university in rural Nova Scotia, a Canadian maritime province. I had a wife and four children (a fifth to come soon) so I looked for a large home. The Scottish people there believed debt was the devil's trap. (Maybe close?) So if they wanted to own a house they saved up for decades until they could pay cash for it.

Being an American with decent credit and less than decent cash, I took the mortgage path immediately. I finally bought a 30 room terraced four-floor mansion on Kings Street, furnished, with ten acres of woods for a back yard. The view from the upper floors was of the Bay of Fundy, a large body of water resembling a great lake. Except it disappeared twice a day, long enough for picnics where the water had been, short ones. The Bay was pulled to the ocean by the most powerful tides on the planet. And then returned.

As you enter the front door, to the left is the library, bookshelves floor to ceiling. And a fireplace. Master bedroom upstairs had a fireplace too as did the living room. The cost of this furnished mansion was a $40,000 dollar mortgage, nothing down.

Still, we had bedrooms to spare. So the university sent me their more challenging students to live in my house, ones not to their taste for dormitory tranquility.

The university had been a Baptist institution and only recently had become part of the Canadian national university system.

Our new roommates were among the brightest more creative people we might have chosen.

They immediately named our home "Morgan House".

The house had ten bedrooms, way more than we needed. One already had a live-in inhabitant. Bob was bald, middle aged, and the town milk man. He lived rent-free in return for being the maintenance and fix-it resource for the house. Bob got up early to do his day job and then his household upkeep chores. By every sunset he was ready for bed. But first he would step out on the front upper floor balcony dressed in robe and slippers to address the Morgan House inhabitants already seated on the lawn terraces below.

Always he gave the same oration: *"The woods are lovely, dark and deep. But I have promises to keep, and miles to go before I sleep, and miles to go before I sleep"*. *Loud applause from the terraces for Bob's heartfelt version of Robert Frost. He would nod happily and then go back into the house over the less than miles to his bedroom.*

The dining room accommodated all house inhabitants. For Thanksgiving we had turkey and ham. The pig supplying the ham had its head left on a corner piece of furniture facing the spacious dining room table. I thought adding a baseball cap and sunglasses brought home the thankful message to the pig meant by Kerouac when he named the title of the Burrough's book *"Naked Lunch"*. Many salutes to the pig were made at that dinner. The pig remained noncommittal.

Asked for the house rules, I said *"You can do anything you want as long as nobody gets hurt"*.

Raised in the town's fundamentalist Baptist tradition where movies and dancing were considered sinful, I was told in a visit 25 years later that this simple sentence was taken to be the revelation of their generation, an opening for the American 1960s to come to their town. In a word: Freedom.

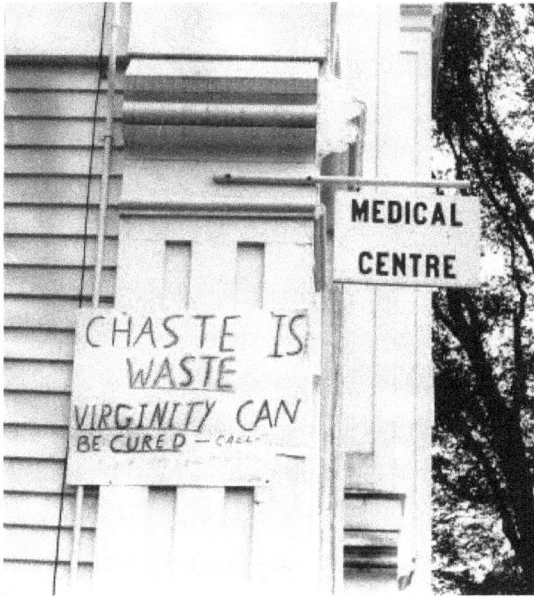

Nor would this freedom ignore its deep religious roots, though not necessarily with respect. I was told by the students early on that American humor leaned too heavily on sex and excretion.

But humor here in this fundamentalist bastion was more religious in essence. Example: *"How was Jesus Christ named? It was the first thing Joseph said when his wife Mary told him she was pregnant."* Then I would be told further, assuming as an American I had to be told, that Mary was the Virgin Mary and never had experienced sex. I added a word: *"Allegedly"*. Confirming their American stereotype.

A year after the American Woodstock, the Canadian Woodstock was held in Nova Scotia. Joan Baez headlined. Instead of the half a million that Woodstock had, true to the smaller Canadian population, we only had a tenth of that at 50,000. Seemed like most stayed at Morgan House for the Concert. In the back of the estate, just before the woods began, was a wooden structure for housing a horse. Tony Harvester's new home.

Animaulda and Charlie

The rent paying students covered our monthly mortgage cost but there was still room for some town people to stay.

The students brought in a laundry woman in her forties. Midge, who was an alcoholic, was soon weaned by students from her drunk persona by substituting marijuana. Midge was a character whose favorite expression was *"Fuckaduck!"*

A local grocery manager moved in, bringing two of his female cashiers as well. Our inhabitants soon exiled the manager and for good reason, but the two cashiers stayed.

One was Animaulda, a self-chosen name. She saw that as the easiest way to tell the world her choices were her own. Let's, for now, refer to her as Anna, her eventual name in a later life.

Charismatic, beautiful, and young, she soon had all in the house but me and the children episodically enjoying the warm summer, usually on our front terraced lawn or roof. Receiving an all-over tan.

A fifteen year old probation placement living with us, Charlie, played loud rock from the same roof.

A shockwave regularly descended over the ultra-conservative neighbors.

By then Anna, raised as an orphan, had at my invitation joined our family. In this role she took on all the household chores, childcare responsibilities, and pet care work as well.

This included Tony Harvester. Feeding, grooming, care for his lame leg until it was no longer lame. In fact it was Anna that had brought me to buy Tony, urging that we save the life of this loving horse. Daily Anna could be seen riding him bareback, no saddle or clothing barrier to the sun needed, a Godiva trot right through the town.

In such a fundamentalist village, there was no prior thought but outrage for dealing with the perception of Morgan House's multi-faceted joyful living. The villagers fell back on open ostracism.

They avoided her and us in the house completely. A universe unto our own, few in Morgan House noticed.

I do recall the university president, a biologist and the first non-Baptist minister to hold that post, calling me into his office re Anna and Charlie.

First he thanked me for the *London Sunday Times* spread just done on my own research and that good press for the university.

Then he brought up Charlie's roof music and Anna's rides through town: *"Dr. Morgan, this is NOT a metropolitan region!"*

No kidding.

Anna continued to exercise Tony in her own creative way.

DJ Charlie still treating the neighborhood to the rock hits of the day from the roof. Neighbors undoubtedly experienced the Beatles, Hendrix, Joplin, and the rest as 'the devil's music'.

The Ghost

The house held joyful parties on weekends.

Not particularly loud but laughter and music did echo down the otherwise quietly devout streets.

Neighbors ranged from tolerant to outraged, though most were just deeply curious.

And then there was the visiting ghost.

In earlier years the house had been used as a long term care facility for the elderly.

At some point on the evening of many parties, an elderly woman would emerge from a wall, view the convivial goings on, shake her head in annoyed disbelief, and then leave through another wall.

This was viewed by most of those at each visitation.

It seemed eventually that I was the only one not to see her.

Until, one sunny day, I was walking down the main street with a group of our resident students. On the way to buy groceries.

Suddenly, they pointed to an older woman across the street. She was walking the opposite way from us, carrying groceries.

Somebody among us yelled: *"That's her! That's our weekend ghost!"*

Sure and certain, everybody agreed.

The woman shook her head in annoyance, as usual, but scurried away as fast as she could.

I made sure we moved on. Leave her alone.

So: not a ghost.

Out-of-body projection?

Curiosity intense among a neighbor?

And, of course, disapproval. Every weekend it would seem.

Then

More than 50 years have passed. Naturally, Tony Harvester has passed as well.

Anna joined us when the family moved to San Francisco. There in the first half of the 1970s, she found an entire city still celebrating the 1960s. Anna's missionary freedom perspective was in every corner.

She thrived there for a time, but missed the wilderness.

Eventually she returned to a very remote corner of Canada. Chose a husband well. With him she raised a family in the fresh air of a very remote forest. When all the children were grown, she remained. Peacefully wild in a happier way. Her missionary days had been left in San Francisco. Now in retirement, her cause is the freedom to love her animals and their humans. That's us too, loving her back.

I live far away from Anna in the state of New Mexico, USA, with my wife of more than thirty years. We are living our own best retirement. Better than possible.

Back to the Monroe Institute OBE Training at the end of the 1970s

That year I was in charge of continuing education for the state of Nevada's mental health staff. I had read that Robert Monroe's training, about to begin, had in preliminary demonstrations brought chronic alcoholics and drug addicts to a healthy abstinence.

Not sure about the out-of-body or OBE stuff but I was intrigued about it all. Further, in its first official training, Jon Voight and Elisabeth Kubler-Ross were in attendance. Staffing for the second training was in process but already the military intelligence people were enrolled.

So I picked that training as my own continuing education choice. Off to Virginia.

OBEs turned out to be real. I didn't get any of my own that time as I was stuck against the very beginning key induction phrase "I am more than my body".

Not stuck there anymore. There is much more to us than can be seen in the body.

Then though, I was at least still able to experience a cathartic healing.

I had been a year going through the most stressful time of my life while still caring for my young children, patients, jobs. I managed okay. Kept it together.

But through the training exercise reaching out for some gift from what we would see as spiritual, I was flooded with joy. And I laughed out loud.

Realizing I had been suppressing laughter, joy, for a year. Cathartic. Thank you Dionysus. Thank you Robert Monroe.

There it was- I could see how that phase of the training might help addicts or anybody else stuck in an unhappy time.

After I thanked Bob and his daughter for this very helpful intervention, they listened to my time statue report on the OBE ghost of Morgan House. Bob thought it was clearly an early understanding of OBE, possibly an explanation of many erroneous ghost sightings.

I told them of the idea I had shared once with a staffer at Nevada's maximum security ward for dangerous mental patients. Mostly serial killers and rapists. Since they were there for up to life, I wondered if the out-of-body training might be a legal way for them to spend their time more fully while incarcerated. Not thinking it through, obviously. The staffer smiled at my idea, saying "Oh, they all do that all the time already!"

More ghost viewings explained?

At this point, Elisabeth got up to go. Plane to catch.

She turned to me and said she had been reading my life extension writings.

I thanked her.

She shook her head no, saying:

"Not a compliment Robert. You are hopelessly stuck in the stage of denial."

Cinnamon Part One

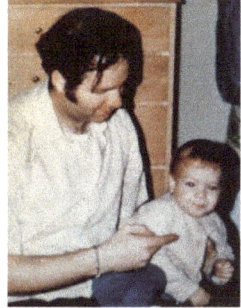

Theme: _Isn't she lovely_ Stevie Wonder

End of the 1960s and into Summer 1972.
Saturday in Ghirardelli Square, San Francisco.

A young man finished his high dexterity juggling act with a bow.

The hundreds of watchers surrounding him, balcony and street, applauded. He suddenly flourished a Lincoln-style hat and tossed it to the crowd. Saying:

> *"Yes, this was a FREE show. Many more to come. But this hat awaits your kind generosity! As you pass it around, well, should you each and every one of you put just ONE DOLLAR in my hat THEN I can go to college." (Pause.) "Wait! If you each put a FIVE DOLLAR BILL in my hat, I won't have to!"*

Smiles and light laughter. Some more donations in a passing hat.

It was a beautiful day. Blue sky and cool sunny.

More kites in the air.

Nonstop performances. Rows of vendors selling surprising things.

Most creative, pleasing. Near Ghirardelli was Aquatic Park, rows of bleachers facing beach and the Pacific Ocean. There was *Santana* rehearsing in its earliest incarnation. Mimes Shields & Yarnell were strolling the sand, shaking hands with tourists.

I carried a four year old girl on my shoulders. My daughter Cinnamon.

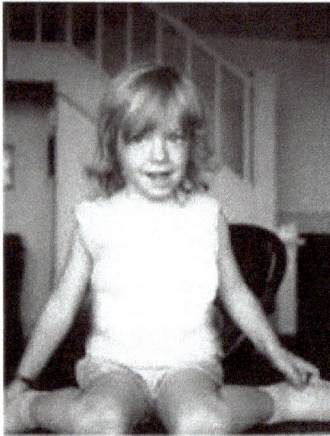

We walked over to a street vendor that was selling his one-page poems for a dollar each. We bought one that Cinnamon liked. I don't recall what it said.

Another vendor was inside a cardboard box with hands sticking out through the front. His sign said "FREE BREAST EXAM".

Near the vendors was a Black man dressed like an African tribesman. He was hiding behind a bush next to the sidewalk. Suddenly he would jump out and wave his spear at a surprised tourist. Racist fantasy brought to life.

People across the street laughed and applauded at this. I hoped he wouldn't pick the wrong one to surprise.

Just outside a stairway to Ghirardelli was a man on the corner who spoke rhymes to entertain all who passed. He made up one for Cinnamon.

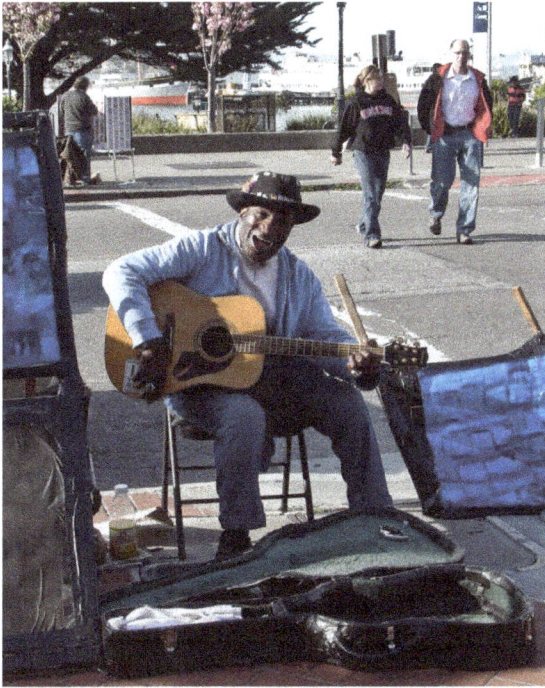

We made our way of course to the namesake store where you could see Ghirardelli chocolate being made.

And eat huge sundaes while there.

A great day for us to remember.

Summer 1990. Saturday in Ghirardelli Square, San Francisco.

The young woman standing next to me was my daughter. She was out of college now and on a music path. Eventually she would take the lead vocal place that Janis Joplin once had with Sam Andrews of *Big Brother and the Holding Company*.

Her own original music was often sweet melodious, a different style but she brought both to vivid life.

172

That day though, to celebrate her graduation from the university in Santa Cruz, we walked to Ghirardhelli Square, remembering our day there 18 years before. Not much had changed. Except there were more kites in the sky.

Some of the same vendors and street actors were still there.

We saw again the man, much older now, selling his one-page poems and still for just one dollar each.

Cinnamon spotted one titled *"Cinnamon"* so she bought it.

I don't recall the author's name now or what it said, but it went something like this:

> **"A Young Knight strode up to my stand**
> **On his shoulders, a child extended her hand.**
> **I yelled "What is your name?" past the noise of a band**
> **She said 'Cinnamon'."**

Cinnamon Part Two

Theme: *Finger Tips* Stevie Wonder

That 'Morgan House' in Nova Scotia had my daughter Cinnamon at its center. She was the only child of pre-school age and got tremendous attention from all the adults in the house.

This was in large part because of her character. Even before she was two, she would refuse to taste an ice cream cone until she knew everybody else had one. One Christmas in Morgan House, I was overheard telling her and her much older siblings that funds were low, so each would get just one present that year. Cinnamon, age 3, stepped forward, saying *"Don't give me any presents then. They can have mine."* Her older brothers and sister thought that was a great idea (I didn't.). The people of the house all soon knew of this. Naturally she was swamped with presents from all of them on Christmas. Altruism can be very rewarding.

Cinnamon was born in 1968 at a very traditional hospital in the Allegheny Mountains. Her mother's anesthesiologist decided to not answer his page until his golf game could be concluded. By the time he showed up, the baby had been delivered and the mother was in shock. He billed me anyway. A bill I intend to ignore until my own game (of life) is over... and not then either.

Once the baby was incubated with her pink blanket, I came to the window for observing the newborn prisoners. Cinnamon was crying.

I asked the nurse to take her to her mother. Nope: not the right scheduled time. I pointed out that she was crying. Nope, said the nurse, the cortex is nonfunctional for the first five years of life, so what I was seeing was only reflex. No feelings or self-awareness until her fifth birthday.

We got out of that place as soon as we could.

Our karmic opportunity happened about 18 months later. My students alerted me. The Saint Bonaventure University faculty member teaching child development, in a classroom I used after her, was a source of the same nonsense: no cognitive functioning before five years of age.

Learning this, I carried Cinnamon into her classroom just as the instructor was finishing her lecture. As I went up front to introduce her to the baby, I slipped Cinnamon some chalk and as I was holding her she began to draw a snowman on the blackboard.

"Why, that's very good!" Dr. Simrall exclaimed. *"Thank you"* said Cinnamon.

"Well, she's 18 months old now. Why not?" I said.

The instructor turned to the class: *"Oh no, that's not normal. She's just very precocious by many years. Some genetic mutation, maybe."*

Me: *"Not at all. We just have always given her a lot of attention and she has responded as any child would."*

The class applauded and Cinnamon smiled.

1972. Living in Diamond Heights, San Francisco. Cinnamon at age four riding her tricycle with eyes shut. Heading for the edge of a cliff.

Eagerly followed by two stepbrothers, ages 13 and 14. Holding their breath, waiting to see if she'll do what they told her to do. Ride as fast as she could with eyes shut until they told her to stop. They had not told her about the cliff drop off, about 40 feet.

Eyes shut but she somehow knew to stop just short of going over the cliff.

Eyes open, she turned her tricycle around and without a word went home.

She survived this too.

At age 8 she had a problem on the rural Colorado school bus. The driver warned her passengers that she would paddle anybody that made a fuss, no matter who started it.

Some boys took advantage of this by pulling the hair of the girls and pinching them. Their victims were afraid to complain for fear of being paddled.

Now a single parent, that summer I enrolled Cinnamon in an adult Aikido class at Aspen. Her Aikido instructor was not much taller than Cinnamon and so chose her as his demonstration partner. He had set aside his prohibition against training children because of her very sunny disposition and eagerness to learn.

By the second week she had learned to fall and roll (saving her grief in a bicycle accident years later). A month in, she demonstrated to me what she had learned. First she did something painless to my wrist that made it difficult to move my hand for a few minutes. Then she proudly challenged me to pick her up which I did easily. Next she shut her eyes and concentrated. *"Pick me up now"* she said.

This time when I tried she seemed stuck to the ground (an Aikido exercise called *anchoring*). She proudly stated that *"four grown men couldn't pick me up today"*.

Clearly she was ready for the boys on the bus.

Not long after this, both Cinnamon and her younger sister Angel gained Rollo May as a godfather. In his *"Days of the Giants"* lecture to a very large California audience, Rollo outlined how the fundamental character flaws that challenged the original greats of psychotherapy led to their contributions. Prior to beginning, he complimented me as *"one of the finest psychotherapists he knew"*. I was stunned by the compliment and very puzzled. I had never been in therapy with Rollo nor had he ever seen me work. I told him afterwards: *"Based on your lecture, I must have overwhelming character flaws."* He replied with a smile, *"I was just judging you by your children."*

Cinnamon went on to get a degree at the University of California Santa Cruz, helped native healer Rolling Thunder recover from a diabetic leg amputation, and helped run a university preschool program. She settled in that Santa Cruz region, now with her own daughter Ava. She writes and performs music.

She still knows how to fall and land on her feet.

Cinnamon Part Three

Theme: *The Dance and the Dream (Isadora)* Cinnamon Camo

The Flower

My daughter Cinnamon and I were close, spending much time together, especially in those years from her birth through to her adolescence. This can be seen in surviving photos of us early on and also with her brother Charlie.

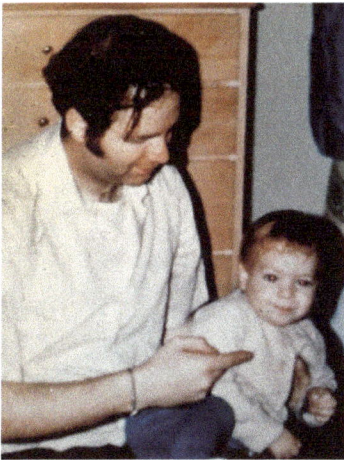

When she was five I took her to Hawaii where we saw a live Tina Turner performance. There she found a family dragon ring (she reminded me that I was born in the Year of the Dragon) that's been worn ever since. A photo was taken of her then, and PermaPlaqued

to a large size for the living room. It was later lost in a fire but here is a photo of her at seven, taken when we lived in Reno.

When she reached her teen years, she often studied the large portrait of her happy five year old self framed there in the living room.

One day she said to me that she was jealous of that little girl in the picture. She didn't like that she had grown out of being that beautiful child. Not her anymore.

I took down the picture and brought it to a mirror where she could see herself next to it.

I explained: *"That was the seed. You are the flower."*

Seemed to help:

A genius-level creative artist, she went on to graduate at a university in Santa Cruz, sang professionally, including with Janis Joplin's former band *Big Brother and the Holding Company,* which became *Sam Andrews and the All Stars*:

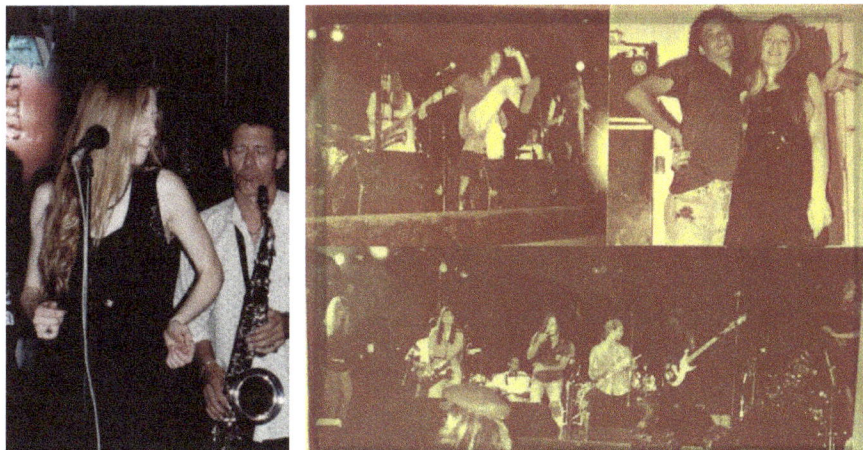

She became an advocate for American Indians, caring for Rolling Thunder in his latter days at the home of Apache Bob (no longer touring with *The Grateful Dead*).

Cinnamon helped run a child care program at the university.

Survived the earthquake that leveled Santa Cruz.

Married a musician and settled into the mountain town of Boulder Creek. She is the mother of a much loved daughter, an appreciated neighbor. A unique glowing flower.

Recorded in a band, *Ohms,* with her husband Ben.

She has a wonderfully creative daughter, one with special requirements, Ava.

Cinnamon, joined by Ava's grandmother Bonnie, devoted herself to
this child thereafter. She knew now that in childhood it was Ava's
turn to be the seed.

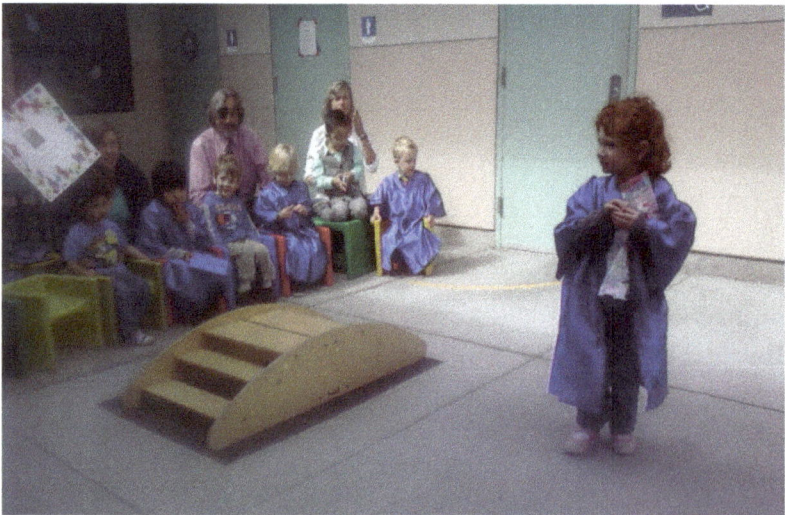

Her flower will be *spectacular*:

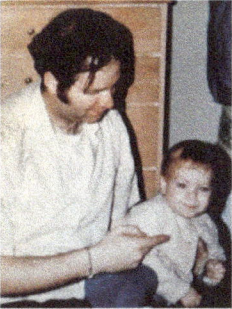

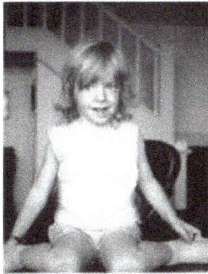

Our Cinnamon

Compassionate Considerate Warm Creative Talented Brilliant Educated Fun Funny Fair Culturally-Competent Singer Dancer Loving Healthy Integrity Honest Mother Daughter Friend Eldest Brave Kind Justice Social-Conscience Lyricist Home-Care Hard Work Reader Genius Inventive Best Adept *StarChild* Sunshine Gold Resilient Strong Relentless Practical Friend Artist Inspiration Kind Eclectic Universe Musician Leader Beautiful Down-To-Earth Safe Moving Vivacious Energetic Graceful Empathic Spiritual Protected.

Always Loved.

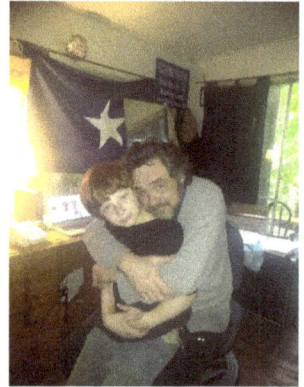

And. In memory of Ben Camo, Ava's father:

1970s

A rose by any other name

Won't know the difference

And neither will they

The Lost and Bound

Theme: *Searchin'* Coasters

Is your husband lost? Never came back last night?

We can help! We are the *LOST AND BOUND.*

We *"Find 'Em and Bind 'Em"* back to you.

In Search of the Journey

Theme: *Searchin'* The Coasters

If you want something you never had before, you must do something you have never done before." - South African Proverb, per Nathan Hare.

I went to a fundraiser at which the guests of honor were Men's Warehouse clothing magnate George Zimmer (*"You'll love how you look; I guarantee it!"*) and actor Leonard Nimoy.

Leonard was promoting his new book, one full of his own creative photography. He had retired from acting and now was enjoying this new career in his final years.

After the guests made their presentations, the whole large group moved into an adjacent room for some food. Leonard stayed behind for a few minutes to autograph copies of his book. I stayed last since I had lacked the foresight to buy a copy for him to autograph.

When we were the only two left in the large meeting room, I told him I had no copy to autograph but I could be his guide to dinner. He smiled and said that would be fine.

He got up and seemed a little unsteady. I put my arm around the small of his back for his stability and we carefully walked out of the room.

Leonard was shorter than I had pictured him and he seemed very frail. I was impressed by how he as a younger actor had carried off the role of a powerful Vulcan. Today he was just Leonard Nimoy, a very fine human in his own right.

He asked me what psychologists like me thought about his "In Search of" television show, possibly wanting to hear nothing further about Star Trek.

I told him I had watched it because of the interesting topic choices and his presentation, all this despite the frustration about it being all search with nothing ever found.

I told him about my former student Roger and his own in-search-of (see next page). He laughed. We made our slow way in search of the dinner.

Which, by the way, we did find.

The miracle is this – the more we share, the more we have.
~Leonard Nimoy

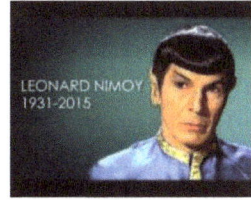
LEONARD NIMOY
1931-2015

The original 'in search of' that I told Leonard about was an exchange with a graduate student I'll call Roger. It was the earliest days of the first freestanding California School of Professional Psychology or CSPP in San Francisco, 1971. In those first days, my class was held on the floor where we all sat on student-chosen harem pillows. Roger was older than most (including me), maybe in his late thirties. He had a goatee and a pony tail, street boots, and a perpetual good-natured smirk. Sitting on his harem cushion, he looked like a life-size garden gnome.

After my presentation on the need for outcome measures of success, Roger ponderously made this statement: *"Life is always just a journey. We may be in search of a destination but this we will not achieve. We must then appreciate that our journey is all that matters."*

Roger then returned to his third cup of coffee, as he sat impressively cross-legged on the cushion. I waited through his fourth cup of coffee while class continued, until he finally arose, turned, and started toward the door.

I asked, *"Where are you going, Roger?"*

Looking somewhat disappointed at my foolish question, *"I'm going to the bathroom!"* he said.

I asked: *"Will you ever get there?"*

Three Weddings

Theme: *"Ain't no sunshine when you're gone"* by Bill Withers

Alternative: *"Ain't no sunshine when you're here either."*

The early 1970s in San Francisco.

The war in Vietnam was still on, extended by Richard Nixon. Those choosing to avoid being drafted to continue the invasion, found creative attempts to dodge this possibility. One of these was to purchase a divinity degree and these were plentifully available.

My own service obligation ended honorably in 1968 but somebody still bought me a doctor of divinity diploma from the *"Church of Universal Brotherhood"*, based in Los Angeles. It had cost $20 and was signed by a *"High Priestess"*.

So I never put this honor on a CV but still posted it in my office while I was Faculty Dean at the California School of Professional Psychology there in San Francisco.

Wedding Number One

Two of my doctoral students were due to graduate. They had planned to get married to each other at that point. Both stopped by in my office and sank together into my spacious most comfortable chair.

(Years later I was asked by a former colleague if I still had that great chair. She said she loved to come by my office and sink into it as long as she could justify. When I told her I had given it away, she demanded to know why. *"People stayed too long"* I explained.)

The young couple, having noted my divinity diploma, asked me if I could officiate at their marriage ceremony. I didn't think my signature on their marriage license would be legal. But, to my surprise, the future bride had looked into this and California recognized that divinity degree as sufficient for the task. Turned out to be true.

The future groom handed me the typed script for the ceremony. They had already written scripts for each of them and another briefer set for me. No thought needed on my part and I liked them both. So when my mouth opened to respond, a Yes came out.

Thorough as ever, the future bride handed me the invitation. It was to take place on Ocean Beach at Sunset the next Saturday. The very place where the famous *Burning Man* extravaganza had first begun.

And so it was.

The sunset was spectacular and the guests friendly.

We read our lines and they kissed. Cheers from guests and a few tourists stopping by.

I signed their marriage license and the event was legalized.

Whew! Seemed to be a contribution I could make.

The next day they gave me a Bonsai Tree in a small pot for my scripted service.

Wedding Number Two

I was given the opportunity as Dean to hire an assistant.

I met with the campus secretaries to see if I should be looking for any specific qualities in candidates. They were unanimous. Noting that they were all female, they really hoped I would hire a male assistant. Better gender balance for the times.

Okay. I was teaching a night class at San Francisco State University. About to graduate there with a psychology B.A. was one of my top students: an immigrant from China named Patrick. He soon was hired as my assistant back at the professional school.

Just prior to that hiring, the president of the system called me into his office for his own advice on hiring an assistant. His advice is still vivid in my memory today.

"Robert, you know I draw the line at any sex between faculty and students. These students are adults and at least as old as most of their teachers but no sex! Same as the need for no sex between therapist and patient- just not ethical! I see you nod agreement." (Now he lowered his voice and moved closer to continue, smiling.) *"I think you may have noticed my assistant and secretaries in the outer office. Kind of attractive aren't they all? THAT is where you go for sex. Fair game. With consent of course. Any questions? Fine. Now go hire your assistant."*

The next day I hired Patrick, very much pleasing the campus secretaries. And for the next four years, the president assumed I was gay. Which he had zero approval for. I let him steam. In the last year he learned finally that I was not gay. I was told that he wondered out loud why I had hired Patrick then.

Patrick didn't stay the full time I was a dean there. But when he left for a better opportunity he asked me for a favor. He wanted to complete his citizenship initiative but would be more likely to succeed if he had an American wife. Now he had found a Japanese American woman, a very good friend, who had agreed to marry him. But just as an act of friendship and not a romantic act. Would I officiate at the marriage and sign their license?

I said that first I needed to talk privately with both bride and groom. He agreed.

In this I was assisted by Ben Tong, then my doctoral student, teaching partner, and eventual lifelong family friend. Ben and I took turns interviewing the potential bride and groom.

Patrick was grateful to his bride for this immigration help. He knew she would like the marriage to last and said he would give it a try.

Dr. Tong and I both found the volunteer bride to be really in love with Patrick and she hoped the marriage might last. We did our best to help her realize that Patrick was not emotionally there yet. We encouraged her to postpone any wedding until they both were committed. But she saw this as her best chance to become the lifelong partner she wanted to be for Patrick. She pleaded with us to go ahead.

It has been said that weddings are a triumph of hope over experience. That was her choice, she knew the risk, and so we went ahead.

The wedding was private. It seemed to go well. Ben Tong recalled: *"I never knew what ultimately became of Patrick's union with his bride. I do vividly recall their imaginative wedding ceremony. Different from conventional practice, the bride had a best man ('the best male friend in my life after my husband,' she proclaimed) and the groom had a counterpart, his best lady. Cool stuff of the '60s/'70s."*

Pat became two new things within the year that followed. He became a citizen. He became an ex-husband.

Quite likely that his ex-wife then wound up marrying her best man after all.

I decided I had done my last marriage ceremony.

Wedding Number Three

My "Doctor of Divinity" diploma was no longer on the office wall.

Despite this, a request walked into my office one day.

She was a recent graduate of the psychology school. In fact I had been Arlene's dissertation chair. I respected her ability, liked her as a new colleague, and was biased to be of assistance.

But she wanted me to perform her marriage ceremony.

In the end of a long discussion, in which I had explained fully why this was a bad idea, the very persuasive Arlene had my consent to go ahead.

This was to be just a small ceremony in her apartment's living room. She had been living there with the potential groom for a few years now with no need for a marriage. But her parents and his as well were somewhat traditional. Arlene knew they would be far less anxious about their interracial relationship if a marriage occurred. No big deal, something just for the comfort of their parents.

We set a date for an afternoon a month later.

A week later she happily announced that both sets of parents would be there. Hers were coming from Mexico and his from Harlem. Anticipating a crowded living room.

I gave it not much more thought until she called me one week before the marriage date.

All four parents were there. Was I going to come in for the rehearsal?

Rehearsal? Turned out that Arlene's parents were devout Roman Catholics and the groom's parents were pastors in their Harlem church.

Alarm bells.

I asked Arlene to graciously decline a rehearsal as we wanted a small family-only living room ceremony in a week. Give the parents some time to catch up on the lives of their adult children. This worked.

Life intervened. The following week was overloaded with my own work and family events. The marriage day arrived unannounced and without my adequate preparation.

I did of course have adequate anxiety. (My daughter tells me that her acting career is enhanced by a little of this. So I hoped.)

I only had a few minutes before leaving for the apartment to choose officiating materials. I took my copy of Arlene's doctoral dissertation. It was about the grandmothers who had come to the USA a century before as very young women. Leading to the birth of a very vibrant Chicano community in San Francisco. The psychology of their success against almost overwhelming odds was well worth the read.

I still needed something more. I scanned my books for something like a bible. The expectations of the traditional Christian parents required that at least. I did have a bible but it was pretty ragged looking. Instead I chose a gold-bound bible-looking volume from the shelf. Turned out it was *"A Passion in the Desert"* by Honoré de Balzac in which a lost French soldier has a romantic affair with a leopard (or lioness in some versions). Ah well, I need not actually read from this book.

Armed with Arlene's hard copy dissertation, black with gold letters on the cover, and the gold-bound French bestiality bible substitute, I arrived at the apartment.

Both sets of parents had been drinking toasts for a while. They were very welcoming in a somewhat solemn way. Impressive people. Just them, the couple to be married and me.

I stood facing the couple to be married, each flanked by their parents.

I chose to begin with honesty.

I acknowledged that I was not a priest or minister but did have legal authority to sign a marriage license and to conduct this ceremony. I let them know how honored I was that Arlene had chosen me for this event, with the groom's consent, though my prior role had only been to Chair her excellent doctoral dissertation as she became a doctor and psychologist. I then held up that very impressive dissertation and opened it to Arlene's dedication, reading: *"La familia lo es todo para la Chicana."*

I continued: *"Or in English 'For the Chicana, Family is everything'. We are gathered here today because this young couple loves their parents. They want them to be happy with this longstanding union in a way that your parental tradition requires. So today what we do here is a celebration of love across two generations. Raising children is far from easy but it is the highest art. Art that finishes itself. As has been successful with these adult children finished and standing before you here."*

I handed the bound dissertation with its gold letters on the cover to Arlene's mother. Then opened the gold book to pronounce the young couple married. Arlene and her husband kissed.

Then all sat down. Silence. The two fathers and the groom's mother had another drink. Arlene's mother was crying.

Was this ceremony too brief or not religious enough? As is said in Singapore: trouble knocking on my door?

Arlene's mother got up and walked over to me.

She said: *"Thank you! That was very beautiful."*

I took a breath of relief. Signed the marriage license.

In a little while I left the happy family with my gold French bestiality bible tucked away in my coat pocket. Before anybody asked to see it.

That was my last time to perform a student wedding. A service discontinued.

End Theme: *"Summertime"* (Willie Nelson/Natalie King)

Or

Wintertime:

"Wintertime, when the weather is freezing

The fish are jumping cuz the water is cold.

Oooeee oooeee"

Batacas

Themes: *Stand* and *Thank You (Falettinme Be Mice Elf Agin)* Sly & the Family Stone; *Stop Draggin' My Heart Around* Stevie Nicks & Tom Petty

Clinical Psychologist George Bach introduced his "Fair Fight Training" couples therapy to our San Francisco professional school in its earliest years. By our year of 1972 it was popular with students and even a few faculty. George demonstrated it's diversity with mixed race couples.

George began his therapy group for couples by telling them to raise their hand when they thought of something that their partner would want to know but they had been afraid to tell them. When enough time had lapsed for group pressure to work, all hands were raised. Then George would say the group could begin: one by one each would tell their secret. Always a lively group.

George had a process for resolution. Each couple would begin negotiation by releasing pent-up hostility. This was done by belting each other with foam rubber covered bats, ostensibly unable to damage participants. These were called Batacas. Once exhausted or timed out, real vocal negotiations could begin. At their close, a sign of affection was expected.

One of my students brought a pair of Batacas into our classroom, explaining they were safe. Another student was Lou Engel, a white martial arts enthusiast married to Brandy, an African-American student. Lou held a Bataca high, gathered his brick breaking Ki, and brought it down with such force that it cracked a wood desktop. Harmless?

After class, Lou asked me if I too pursued a discipline in the martial arts. I was hearing this term 'martial arts' for the first time, much less a required affiliation. So I just shared that I followed a non-violent path, a discipline I named *Martial-Mellow*. Best roasted on a non-foam stick over a fire.

Followed next the generational delight of Bruce Lee movies. All was soon made clear.

I was at the time involved in a troubled marriage, well within its final years. She eventually brought home a pair of Batacas so we could release our hostility. Remembering Lou's demonstration, I declined. But she insisted. Now I did not want to hit her nor did I desire being hit. This I said.

But she ignored this and attacked with her Bataca.

My solution in the moment was to treat this as a martial arts exercise (by then I was hooked). I would neither hit her with the Bataca nor allow her to land any hits on me. In those, my young days, I had more speed than most.

So as hard and fast as she attacked, I blocked it every time. Neither of us was ever hit. After many frustrating minutes for her, she threw her Bataca down.

I let George know that my in-the-moment technique, as any psychologist might have expected, raised hostility exponentially. I also told him about Lou Engel's demonstration. He shrugged.

Never saw Batacas again. Or George for that matter.

He died in Los Angeles in 1986.

But no evidence that it was from Batacas.

Easter Story

Themes: *Low Rider* War; *Perfect Angel* Minnie Ripperton,

It was the day after Easter Sunday. San Francisco.

Andy brought me to his friend Felicia's house for an afternoon break from work.

A time so laid back and wonderful that it still glows in my memory.

Felicia could have been Andy's female twin. Both highly creative, kind, brilliant, welcoming, fun. And proudly African American.

She looked like Minnie Ripperton and that was the first music she played for us as we sprawled on her living room carpet. It was Ripperton's breakthrough album.

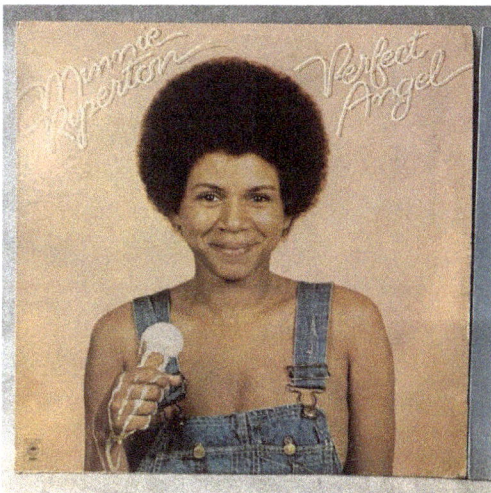

What a range of voice!

Plus the snacks helped.

Our appreciation hunger was likely enhanced by inhaling the "*incense*" in the room which added to the next breakthrough album we heard together:

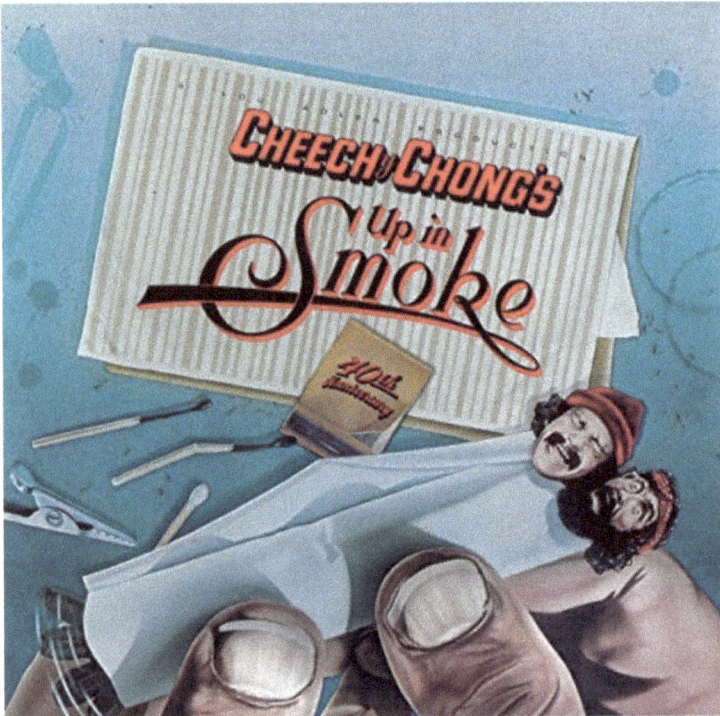

Felicia had a phone call just after that. At her end, she just said *"Oh you have the wrong number! The wrong Felicia. I'm Felicia Newme! Okay. No problem. Bye."*

Soon Felicia explained that her debts had become overwhelming. Threats and calls from collection thugs seemed nonstop. Andy Curry had reminded her that she was a creative star, told her that she should sleep on the problem and wake up with the answer. This she had done and it worked!

She legally changed her last name to *"Newme"* and, naturally, began as her new debt-free self. In that magic San Francisco temporal geography, it had worked. For a couple of months already since her name change, Felicia Newme had been happy enjoying her fresh persona, now celebrating this with us.

Sometime later, after both albums were done, Felicia noticed what seemed like a small deep bite mark on Andy's arm. Demanded explanation. Hoping it was from passion, she said. An Andy Curry story to be told.

Andy was a global expert on the social process of groups, an expertise he lived. With just his social work credential, he was a top faculty member in psychology's first free-standing professional school. And the most loved.

There he added theatricality. Began the *Tantric Feets Dance Ensemble* for the students. Founded the campus newspaper as the *Freedom from Disabling Pathology Gazette*. He had studied with Gestalt psychiatrist Fritz Perls and many other psychology greats, teaching that psychology history from personal experience.

So Felicia knew that any story from Curry would be an event.

He rose to the occasion. Might as well have been standing on a stage in an auditorium or so it seemed as the living room faded. Felicia had dimmed the lights so Andy stood under the only bright one.

He explained, most theatrically, that he had been walking in Golden Gate Park the day before and had come upon a young white family celebrating Easter there with a picnic.

The parents signaled for him to come sit with them on their blanket silently as their little boy was covering his eyes, waiting for an Easter surprise.

An overflowing Easter basket had just been set in front of the child. Andy sat quietly behind the basket, glad to incorporate this sweet event into his walk.

The boy was told he could take his hands away now and see his Easter present. Which he did.

Full of joy he ran past the basket and bit Andy hard on the arm.

Andy mimed the event effectively until Felicia finally exclaimed *"But WHY?"*

Andy had been waiting for that.

Solemnly he intoned, voicing the mother's apology with undoubted accuracy:

"Oh! We're so sorry for that. See he's still crying. He just whispered to me that he thought that big chocolate rabbit was for HIM."

Afterthought

Then and now celebrities are at times memorialized in chocolate so that they can be symbolically bitten, consumed, and without pain:

Benedict Cumberbunny

Kind of like in church when the Eucharist wafer is consumed with wine to represent dining on the body and blood of Jesus.

Better when just symbolic said Andy.

Trust
(1944, 1972, 1996)

Theme: *Smiling Faces* Undisputed Truth/Temptations

Trust is essential for any relationship to survive. Children need trustworthy parents, good marriages require trustworthy partners, staff deserve trustworthy administrators. Effective police departments must earn the trust of their community. Trust is especially important, sometimes life or death, for a doctor's patient. Magnified when the patient is a child.

Dr. David Cheek was just beginning to be recognized as a master hypnotist in 1972. One of my graduate students, Gene Orro, gave me his phone number and recommended I hire him for a hypnosis workshop. I had already decided that psychology's first free-standing school of professional psychology should offer hypnosis as a first year core skills class. So I called.

He had a San Francisco gynecology and obstetrics practice not far from us. He had already made a mark with his respectful client-centered hypnosis approach. Automatic consent or dissent signals from designated fingers for every step.

He agreed to do an all day workshop so we set a time and date. But he refused to take any pay. Said we were new, just getting started, and, besides, he was happy to train psychologists in his approach. Medical doctors were uninterested so far, though nurses and dentists were on board.

I told him I would be there at the workshop along with my students. As it was a very large group, I suggested he ask for me before the workshop to sign some papers. Though I was the Dean, I was the same age then as my students and, being in San Francisco, dressed the same. I started to describe myself but he declined, since he would know which one I was soon enough.

We assembled for the workshop and waited. Just at the exact time it was supposed to begin, Dr. Cheek, confident in a three piece suit, walked in. With a friendly smile, he said it was time to begin. Said he would catch the Dean at the break.

He arranged us to stand in a large circle, maybe two dozen of us. He had brought enough pencils for each of us to hold one at arm's length. Then he had us, now with finger signing permission, go into a light trance. Eyes shut. We were told that we would know when this auto-hypnosis was ready by realizing that the pencil had fallen to the floor.

When we were asked to open our eyes, all the pencils were down. Except mine. I was still holding it in my outstretched arm.

David walked up to me and said *"Nice to meet you Robert. So you're the Dean."*

David later told me that I had dropped my pencil at the same time as everybody else but I had bent down and picked it back up. I had no memory of doing this so the trance had worked.

In the workshop afternoon, David divided us into pairs. Each would take turns standing straight and then falling backwards so as to be caught by the partner. This was called a trust exercise. I caught my partner easily. But I could not (with psychologists that meant *'would not'*) fall backwards. With any partner.

So David chose to use me to demonstrate his trauma resolution technique. He usually did this early trauma memory recovery hypnosis for his female patients, going as far back as needed, even to birth or the trimester before. For me I only went as far as age three. This was the trauma time statue I revisited that day with David.

I was on my way to the hospital to have my tonsils removed. Fix my sore throat. This was okay because I had been raised and praised for being tough in such situations. And I trusted these giants called doctors. They would make me well, just fine. Then I was in a hospital bed, ready. In walked these giants (to me) in white coats. The one in front said "Hello Bobby. We are going to take you now to have a nice ice cream cone. For your sore throat. Isn't that nice?" I hadn't expected this, but sure! They put me on top of something with wheels and rolled me into a dimly lit room. Lifted me onto a table and strapped me down. No ice cream in sight. Put a mask over my face that began hissing. I couldn't speak and they couldn't hear me. They had LIED to me. I was good at following what a doctor told me. Pain didn't slow me down. Why the ice cream lie? Doctors weren't supposed to lie to children, to me! I got really angry. I figured out that the hissing mask was supposed to put me to sleep. So I fought it.

I still was awake and glaring. They gave me more hissing in the mask. Still awake, eyes open. More hissing. At some point. I finally passed out. When I woke it was another day. My mother was there looking worried. Said I had been asleep for three days. Too much hissing in the mask. Said finally now I could go home. Still no ice cream.

David's intervention was helpful to me though not 100%. I had after age three been damaged eventually in various falls and still was cautious about falling. I as an adult knew by then that not every doctor or not every other person we meet in life could be trusted. More honor to those who could be.

Bringing this trauma to light though may have explained many things still true in my life. My lifelong work of preventing iatrogenic practice, the doctor's mistakes, may be an outcome. Seeking the final end of the demonstrably destructive electroconvulsive shock treatment a prime example. Books along these lines surfaced between 1982 and 2005 with more to come. They should have given me that ice cream cone.

David Cheek's workshop was a big success. The students used self-hypnosis regularly. Overcoming test anxiety, fulfilling skills, speed reading. Research, and many fresh creative avenues. On graduating, they could apply the Cheek method to their practice, for the great benefit of their patients. Today, it's prevalent for hypnotists everywhere.

Since David's office was close to my work, many secretarial staff were his patients. You could tell by their twitching fingers which let me know agreement or the opposite independent of what was said. They also told me that, as the years rolled by, David never raised his $10 an hour fee for them. His methods saved many lives and restored a future to many more.

Cheek and I became close friends. It was not the case that he would join me in the 21st century. He remains a heroic time statue in the 20th.

Let's go forward 24 years from that day in 1972 to his future 1996 memoriam. We'll better understand who he was. And in that time who he will always be.

In memoriam:
David B. Cheek, M.D.

written by: Dabney M. Ewin

David Bradley Cheek died on June 12, 1996 at the age of 84, after a short bout with lymphoma. He was an early member and the sixth president of the American Society of Clinical Hypnosis.

Born in Singapore in 1912, he was the grandson of a medical missionary to Siam. He had wide interests in all life forms and their origins. He studied first geology and paleontology, then premed at Harvard. His education was interrupted by tuberculosis, and he subsequestly received his medical degree from the University of California, San Francisco. He completed his internship and residency in obstetrics and gynecology at John Hopkins in 1945. It was about that time when he met William Kroger, who was doing pioneering work with hypnosis in gynecology and demonstrating the use of hypnosis as the sole anesthetic for obstetrical deliveries and major surgical procedures. This began a lifelong interest in hypnosis and the obvious as well as the subtle influences that subconscious ideas and imprints have on body physiology.

Cheek recognized early the difference between ideomotor signals (a form of affect-driven body language) and the usual conversational hypnosis. He used ideomotor signals to uncover birth imprints, sounds heard under general anesthesia, and subconscious fears causing spontaneous miscarriages, none of which where available with conversational hypnosis. Cheek is to ideomotor as Erickson is to indirect suggestion. His last book, *Hypnosis: The application of Ideomotor Techniques* (1994) reviews his years of experience and details his techniques. A clinician's hypnosis library may be deemed incomplete without it.

He co-authored two books, *Clinical Hypnosis* with Leslie LeCron, and *Mind-Body Therapy: Methods of Ideodynamic Healing in Hypnosis* with Ernest L. Rossi. He contributed chapters to six other books and published 43 articles on psychosomotic medicine.

Dave always had a curious and open mind, even traveling to Brazil seeking to understand the mysteries of the spiritist healers there. He observed animals and studied Volgyesi's work with animal hypnosis. He was a pioneer, a doctor's doctor, and a wonderful teacher. His cheery smile and warm caring will be missed by all of us who knew and worked with him. We extend our condolences to his wife Dolores and the rest of his family.

> *"He was a pioneer, a doctor's doctor, and a wonderful teacher."*

Sources

Cheek, D. B. (1968) *Clinical hypnotherapy*. New York: Grune & Stratton.

Cheek, D.B. (1993) *Hypnosis: the application of ideomotor techniques*. New York: Allyn & Bacon.

Cheek, D. B. & L. LeCron (1968) *Clinical hypnotherapy*. New York: Grune & Stratton.

Morgan, R.F. (1982, 2005). *The Iatrogenics Handbook: A Critical Look at Research & Practice in Helping Professions*. Toronto: Morgan Foundation.

Morgan, R.F. (1999). *Electroshock: the Case Against*. (With Peter Breggin, Leonard Frank, John Friedberg, Bertram Karon, Berton Roueche) Albuquerque, NM: Morgan Foundation. (Chapter IV reprinted in Brent Slife's *Taking Sides: Psychological Issues, 13th edition,* Guilford, CT: McGraw-Hill/Dushkin, 2004 and in Richard P. Halgin's *Taking Sides: Abnormal Psychology, 2nd edition,* Guilford, CT: McGraw-Hill/Dushkin, 2002. (First edition: *Electric Shock*. Toronto: IPI Publications, 1985.)

Morgan (2012). *Trauma Psychology in Context: International Vignettes and Applications from a Lifespan Clinical-Community Psychology Perspective*. Santa Cruz, CA: Morgan Foundation.

The Confidentiality Trap

Themes: *Sound of Silence* Simon & Garfunkel/Johnny Cash; *That's When Your Heartaches Begin* Andy Kaufman

1975. My first day as the Chair of a psychology department in a small state Colorado university.

The rugged weather included drought and sand storms. Maybe that's why, from the outside, the university looked like a cement castle fortress.

Local saying: *"Feast or Famine, Flash Flood or Drought, Take your Pick, We Got 'em All."*

The department had a dozen faculty. Most were not talking to the others. Lots of barely suppressed anger, suspicion, upset stomachs.

I was replacing a past Chair of ten years in that role. He seemed a particularly friendly and decent man. With ears stuck so far out to the side that I thought to myself he would be a great listener.

I think he was the first I heard to say that the title of "Chair" meant he could be sat on. And as he shared his memories, I thought that remark summarized his time there pretty well.

He was not a clinical psychologist. But he did understand confidentiality. Or so he thought. Told me that eventually everybody he supervised had come to him to complain about somebody else. Always swearing him to secrecy first. Since his promise bound him to confidentiality, absolute in his interpretation, he felt bound to not resolve any of these disputes. Not that long then that none of his faculty knew what had been said about them. Bright people have great imaginations. The atmosphere grew in hostility. The poor department Chair was overwhelmingly weighed down with the chains of secrets.

Had he done the clinical training, he might have learned that only clergy and attorneys have a near absolute legal confidentiality privilege. Psychologists though have very clear legally mandated exceptions to confidentiality in their clinical practice which are to be clarified with clients, usually in writing and with their signature, before beginning any therapy.

But this situation was not in therapy. It could happen in any exchange between people anywhere.

"I want to tell you something very important. Do you promise to never tell anybody what I'm going to tell you?"

The nice Chair had always agreed.

What else could he say? Maybe this.

"No." or *"I'll use my best judgment. Depends what you have to say."*

I met with the past Chair and all the department faculty.

Just said to them *"If you come to me with a complaint about anybody else in this room, I want you to have told that person face-to-face first. If that can't be resolved, I might meet with both of you. I definitely do*

NOT promise you confidentiality, but I can promise I'll use my best judgment about any action I subsequently take. And I'll tell you. Put simply 'No more secrets between us'."

Within a few days we had a more relaxed and peaceful group.

The outside storms, sand or otherwise, never let up though.

Puppy Unleashed

Theme: *Walk on the Wild Side instrumental* Jimmy Smith

As to a Siberian Husky named Chort, he followed my Golden Rule of Proportionality, solving more problems than he created.

Time is an important dimension in applied psychology. To psychoanalytic psychologist Dr. Al Talkoff, it was a key issue for psychotherapy. In fact he was teaching a course for clinical doctoral students at psychology's first free standing psychology school entitled *"Where do you put your clock?'* I never did ask Al where he thought the clinician's clock should go, but I eventually decided it had to be where both therapist and client could see it. The year was 1971.

The 13 of us hired as the first core faculty at the California School of Professional Psychology's San Francisco campus, including Al, had no core curriculum yet. Our students were often older than we were and had only come in from an active MA-level practice to secure a PhD. Consequently, faculty and students collaborated to develop courses amplifying what they already knew and also what they needed to learn.

This led to substantial creativity and experimentation. I was particularly pleased with my invitation to David Cheek MD to teach hypnosis to beginning students (and for us faculty too). Often held as a last year elective in today's doctoral programs, if there at all, David showed it to be of great value as a basic skills course. Students used it for speed reading, enhanced comprehension, reduced test anxiety, and a helpful tool for client success. They also learned, importantly, how not to use it since altered states can make patients under stress very suggestable.

In fact, David demonstrated that hospital operations can be deadly with negative medical staff comments or helpful with positive ones. Patients under these conditions typically develop involuntary hypnotic states. So, all in all, the placement of hypnosis training and other human potential offerings at the beginning of the program were of great value.

Timing again.

The Early Years: Puppy Unleashed

Dr. Al Talkoff (a great last name for a psychoanalyst?) employed his sense of timing to have me solve a domestic problem of his. He invited me and my young children to come over and meet his canine family. Al bred Siberian Huskies as a major hobby. I was leery of bringing my children to this since we already had two cats.

I had a feeling the children would not want to leave without a puppy. Al guaranteed me that he would not sell me a puppy so we went.

There it was that we first met Chort.

He was a beautiful male Siberian Husky puppy with two-toned blue and brown eyes. Yet he was not one that Al could show, sell, or breed. This puppy had one testicle undescended which, apparently in the dog show world, ruined his value.

Further, according to Dr. Talkoff, the puppy was "overcompensating" for this missing testicle by behaving in a very "oversexed" manner. Once he was separated from the female puppies he had begun mounting the males.

Now San Francisco, then and now, is very comfortable with bisexuality. But for this psychoanalytic psychotherapist such behavior was less than welcome.

And there was more. This puppy, like so many Siberian Huskies, was an escape artist.

And a very successful one. He had learned to spring locks and gnaw through cages until Al despaired of ever containing the libidinous puppy.

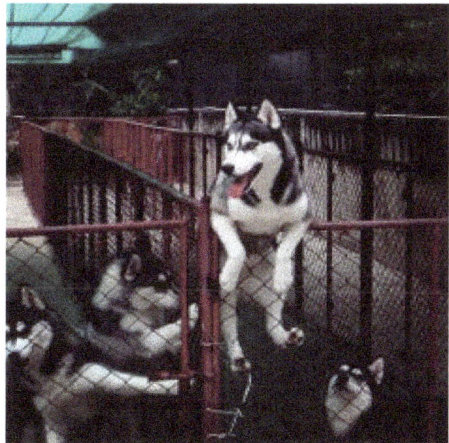

So he named him "Chort" which, Al confided, was the Russian word for Devil.

We took the devil home with us but free of charge as Talkoff had promised.

Chort seemed to understand immediately that he was now part of a family pack, despite our many non-canine shapes and smells.

To our pleasant surprise he got along with, well, tolerated the young cats already part of our family group.

More important than that, he understood immediately that he was to protect our human puppies, playing with them somewhat but always keeping a watch on their wellbeing.

This was very important in an era when young children were free on weekends to play in a not always safe city.

This was especially so for the youngest ones including an infant girl, and then later when she was a toddler.

I established my alpha role with Chort early on. Not only was I the one to feed him during his earliest days with us, including treats for good behavior, but I was also the one to negotiate his freedom.

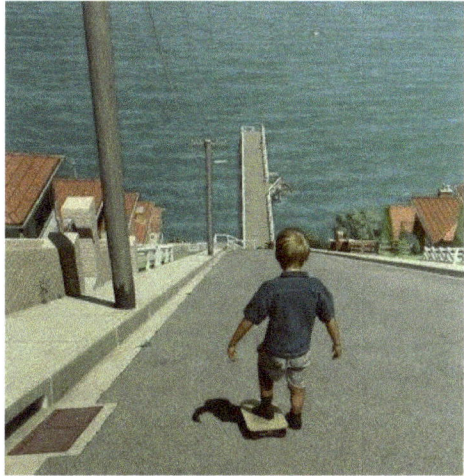

Chort was superb at reading body language and, in my failure to learn formal sign language, I had developed some fluency in just plain gestural communication, later enhanced by body language expert Dr. Ernst Beier.

On our first walk together, I removed Chort's leash and signaled that he was to stay next to me.

When he began to stray, I held out and waved the leash: he came back.

Except for one rare circumstance years later (discussed following), from then on he always walked free of leash. He thrived and grew.

Puppy unleashed, he was free to explore San Francisco.

The Urban Chort

Now a young Canine-American, he roamed the city for adventure, as most dogs domestic and feral (including the tie-dyed ones) did in those days, but he always returned in time for dinner.

Apparently through some Skinnerian event, he had learned to ring doorbells.

I could imagine the surprise in some homes when they opened their door to a wolf-like animal that calmly entered and helped himself to goodies.

Once he came home with a cooking pan filled with chicken, handle firmly in his teeth.

One of the children wanted him to bring back toys while an older one thought jewelry might be nice.

Then I got calls on an election day that he was following voters to join them in their booth to see what they were doing in there. He was retrieved.

Down the street from us was a cement front porch slab on which two large dogs, let's call them Ma and Pa Barker.

Plus a posse of several smaller pet canines growled and menaced the children as they walked to and from school.

So Chort and I took a walk that led us by them.

True to form, as we approached at a distance, a cacophony of barks met us. Then all stopped suddenly as Chort came into closer view. Huskies have jaws like Jackals, very powerful. The Siberian varieties have speed and intelligence plus a certain confidence bordering on royalty.

By now we were close and all the porch growlers had grown silent, frozen in place.

This may be too anthropomorphic for some, but Chort definitely laughed silently.

He ascended the cement platform and strolled among the dogs, still as statues. Then Chort lifted a leg and marked the Barkers as his territory. Finally, my canine samurai returned to our walk, the job well done. Silence followed us from behind.

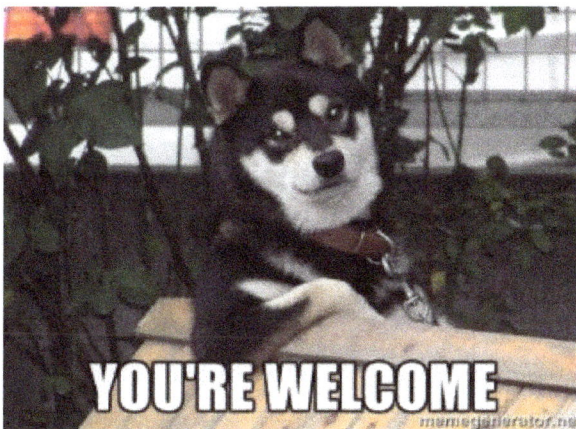

YOU'RE WELCOME

The Middle Years: Salute to the High Desert Regions of the World

At the end of four years we moved to the high desert of Pueblo West, Colorado.

I was a psychology department head at a university 20 miles from our new very remote home. The nearest visible neighbor was a home in the far distance. The rest was open land, including rattlesnakes, most dangerous when shedding their skin (and visibility) but also attracted to any open water. We had a swimming pool in the back yard, the only outside water for many miles.

Our neighborhood was also inhabited by coyotes, scorpions, nightshade, and also the tarantulas that roamed in October to mate.

Every May there was a mass infestation of moths, so dense their bodies were still being found months later, even inside desk drawers and glove compartments.

But between Chort and the growing family of the original two city cats (now more than a dozen and counting) they kept the outside area around the home free of varmints. A delicate ecology but it worked. Now free to roam as outside residents, the cats expanded their population with every new generation: youngest stayed in place while the oldest ventured farther.

Chort was allowed in-house privileges when the weather warranted it, but normally preferred the free outdoors. He gathered together bushes in a shady place far from the house for his own excretory contributions.

We considered this his way to copyright his puppy short stories and adventures for other dogs within olfactory range.

The fenced acre around the house was his territory to guard, although he left it at will to explore, walk the girls to their school bus, meet them when the bus returned, and never went so far he could not respond to my calling his name.

Chort was now an adult of both years and experience. Also with immense self-confidence, this based on years of mastering any and every challenge. Except for that first night in our new high desert home.

The sky was open and beautiful. Sunsets were spectacular, often rivaling the beauty found in the Pacific.

Following a sunset, the moon could dominate the sky. On a moonless night there would be dramatic sparkles of stars and other celestial art. Unless, of course, a night without a moon was overcast.

It was on one such dark moonless night, that first night in our new home, that the sky was too overcast to see any stars. So naturally, visibility on the ground was nil.

Once the children were asleep, their mother suggested we take a walk around the desert block, possibly an hour round trip. She held the flashlight and Chort led us on the path.

He was fearless as ever. Until... he whined, put his tail between his legs, and backed away to move closer to us. This was the first and the only time I had ever seen him frightened.

I turned to ask my companion what she thought had spooked him. Only to see that she and my flashlight were already halfway back to the house.

I decided Chort must have a very good reason, so I turned and walked back toward the receding rays of my flashlight, the husky, fearless again, leading me toward home. Afraid or not, he had stayed with me. But he was also delighted to lead us in an apparently much safer direction.

He had been right. The next day I found the tracks of an adult mountain lion and her cubs directly in the path we had been on.

He did soon get a new opportunity to excel. On a daylight walk about a mile from our home, we saw two huge farm mastiffs in the distance, also roaming free. Once they scented and saw us they charged.

The two distant dots fast came close enough to see clearly that they were at least twice Chort's size and clearly ready to bite. I got ready to defend myself with a walking stick, but no need. I hadn't even seen Chort leave my side, but there in the distance he was racing toward them. Then there was a cloud of dust.

As I was running to help him, Chort emerged from the cloud head held high, almost prancing.

The two mastiffs were running away from us, one limping.

As we moved through the four seasons, Chort became ever more at home, seemingly ready even to co-exist peacefully with any willing high desert predator.

I imagined him in winter with a friendly bear.

Chort Finds Romance

Then there was his love life.

At first it was a beautiful thing to see.

One particularly gorgeous female golden Collie was brought home often by Chort, usually to lounge by the swimming pool. Once she was running after him and slipped, falling into the deep end of the pool. Chort had never shown any interest in this domestic body of water. Now though, he jumped in after her and floated her to the shallow end where he and I could retrieve her.

Note: My daughter, psychologist Dr. Angel Morgan, added another memory I had forgotten. She recalled this from when she was five years old: *"I remember a handful of the kittens once walked right into the pool. Without question Chort jumped into the pool after them, and swam them to safety on the deck one by one by their scruffs. We were like, 'Our hero! Good job, Chort!' and I imagined him thinking, 'Yeah. No problem. Don't make a fuss.' And then strutting off like, 'I know I'm a badass.' "*

Huskies, like wolves, tend to develop lifelong pair bonds with a mate. But Chort remained unattached, except for brief liaisons with many different partners. Which led to his next major problem.

Our only neighbor down the road had a female Saint Bernard.

She was a source of his income as a breeder of purebred Saint Bernard puppies, valuable sales in that region. Whenever she was in heat, he would rent a Saint Bernard male and generate more revenue.

One day he called to let me know his female was in heat and I needed to keep my oversexed Siberian Husky away. He promised that, even though he loved dogs, he would sadly need to shoot Chort should he try to take advantage and mount his furry meal ticket at that delicate time.

I believed him capable. I told him to keep her inside the house then.

Just to make sure, I did my best to let Chort know he had to stay away from that house.

Chort understood "no" and understood my gesture to the house. He also was clear in his body language that he was not in agreement, even quietly taking a few steps in that wrong direction. I tried to get across the idea of being shot but that was either too abstract or too unconvincing. After all, the scent of a female like the Saint Bernard in heat was the real Call of the Wild for free roaming Chort.

So, gesturing my "no" again and my sadness, I reluctantly put him on a leash and tied it to a fence post at the front of the house. He was stoic about it as he took on the stance of a Ulysses lashed to the mast so as to resist the song of the Sirens. Then I left for work 20 miles away.

On return I saw a very tired Chort leaning against the fence post, his fur all tangled. Around him was a mixture of blood and multiple Coyote paw prints. Some pack had taken advantage of his lack of mobility.

Chort had only a few scratches but it was clear that I could not leave him so vulnerable again. The lack of dead coyotes suggested they might come back.

Explaining by gesture again that he was in trouble if he went to the neighbor's home, I set him free. He settled that evening for a quiet meal, some petting by family, and a good night's sleep.

The next day I set out once again for work. Chort walked the girls to their school bus as he always did. On coming home, my neighbor was waiting for me.

He had kept his Saint Bernard inside his house just as I had wanted him to. But then, in the afternoon, his doorbell rang. Once he opened the door, Chort flashed by and mounted the female before our neighbor could stop him.

Rather than shoot our dog he had a monetary alternative. So I agreed to compensate him for the lost litter opportunity and even take one of the puppies.

Chort was left to live another day, free and wanton.

Saint Bernard dogs are strong and bred to be fully focused on one task at a time (guaranteeing they won't drink the rum themselves while on rescue trips). Sadly the female puppy had her father's combat skills and her mother's mission focus. Might have worked out if it had been the other way around. As sweet as she was, she still decided it was her goal to liquidate the kittens. After the second one, I had to find another home for this puppy before her serial killing could continue.

A New Wolf

In our second year of high desert living, Chort became even more valuable. We were halfway between the state prison and the state mental hospital's maximum security wing. Periodic escapes and subsequent road barricades were far too frequent. His vigilance was an impressive safety factor. Visitors from Canada had to stay in their car for hours until I came home from work to welcome them. They said a wolf had kept them in there. I introduced them to Chort, not really a wolf, yet, and then they got along fine.

Feeding Chort had now been delegated to my teenager, the eldest of the three daughters remaining at home. She, at that age, had other more imperative interests to address and apparently Chort began missing meals. One evening I saw Chort dragging home an opened 10 pound bag of dog food. I asked my teenager when she had fed him last. "What day is this?" she responded. Oh.

I began again doing the feeding. But it was no longer enough. During his weeks of sporadic home meals, Chort had learned to live off the land, and not just for bags of dog food. Soon there were stories of some wild wolf taking down sheep and goats in the regions farms at night.

One weekend afternoon I decided to take Chort with me to visit friends on a nearby farm we had visited once when we first moved there. In an earlier visit, the livestock had ignored Chort and he reciprocated. This time when they saw him, the livestock panicked.

Chort was calm but that smile of his was there again.

Circumstantial evidence but...

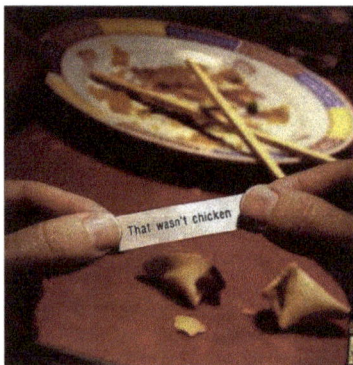

That wasn't chicken

Chort's Latter Days

About then, a series of life changing events happened.

For one, I had been instrumental in getting the state mental hospital to stop giving weekend passes to maximum security former rapists and serial killers which, as you might gather, was not popular with them. My ability, even with the formidable help of Chort, to protect the children was increasingly less apparent. I also had just become a single father with daughters to care for.

I took a year off to consider the choices.

I decided to look at a university job in Perth, Australia. But taking Chort with us to Australia would have been an overwhelming hardship for him. Legally, He would have had to be confined to a kennel prison for months in the process. Years to a dog already now in midlife. Instead, one of my students agreed to take care of Chort in our absence.

The university job looked well worthwhile but their academic year was the calendar year. So I would have had to wait nine months to begin and collect a first paycheck, hard as the sole support of a small family. We stayed and considered. It was there, sitting with three daughters, that we all first saw the *Fiddler on the Roof* movie. About three daughters leaving home.

Eventually though, an opportunity arose to come back to the United States and run professional mental health continuing education in Nevada. This would be in a system that was accidentally progressive and way ahead of its time: psychiatrists would not work for the lower state wages so psychologists and social workers were running things. This too would be a wait, but not as long.

We had enjoyed Australia but in the end we chose Nevada. When returned to our former high desert setting, much time had passed. Experiential dog years for Chort. My student had passed Chort on to live with his mother in the city of Pueblo, a kind woman the Husky had in time bonded with.

She was an elderly woman with no other caring companion. Chort was no longer young himself. Given the far too short lifespan of Chort's species and the similar remaining life expectancy of his new human, they seemed temporally matched. They certainly both were content to grow older together.

So we accepted this new arrangement and wished that these last days be their best for them both.

Final Note

If Einstein and Vonnegut were right, time is a place. If so, then every moment of our life is always there, vibrant in those coordinates of time and space.

It follows that each day of our existence creates these eternal statues in time.

Some of these sculptures are best forgotten, others well worth remembering.

This creation is our temporal art.

Chort was clearly a very fine artist.

Should life ever give us another chance to add a Siberian Husky to our family, I would welcome this.

But only if this intelligent, resourceful, and loving being can each and every day still roam free.

A puppy forever unleashed.

"Here is a new day, fresh and untouched. What will we do with it?"

- Native American Church

Wisdom

Theme: *Custer Don't Ride Good Any More* Buffy Sainte-Marie with Johnny Cash

When I was in my thirties, I co-hosted a university workshop in Pueblo, Colorado. It was about ethnocentric responses when contacting diverse cultures, and post-contact survival methods. My co-host was distinguished psychologist and American Indian educator Dr. Arthur McDonald. Our attendees included diverse faculty from the Pueblo region. For them they knew that this was personal and important. In our last session, I shared my summary of Dr. McDonald's remarks in a chart:

Ethnocentric Response Levels (Worst to Best)

Annihilation	(Genocide, Holocaust, "Ethnic Cleansing")
Evacuation	(Deportation, "Removals")
Isolation	(Ghettos, Concentration Camps, Involuntary Reservations)
Assimilation	(Cultural Removal)
Celebration	(Intact culture welcomed with its gifts appreciated)

Art McDonald spoke after my presentation as follows: *"We believe that wisdom only comes with age. Wisdom is not likely before 60. When a man who has not yet lived past his 30s says something like this that sounds like wisdom, we consider it coincidence."*

Present day: *"Art, we're in our 80s now. Did I miss it?"*

Saying Nothing

Themes: *Sound of Silence* Simon & Garfunkel/Johnny Cash; *I've Got Plenty of Nothing* Gershwin's Porgy & Bess;

> *Do not go gentle into that good night,*
> *Old age should burn and rave at close of day;*
> *Rage, rage against the dying of the light.*
>
> –Dylan Thomas 1974

Leon was a psychiatrist at San Francisco's Center for Special Problems (CSP).

He wasn't viewed as belonging to the group of psychiatrists working there.

Instead he was a member of the group of individuals that belonged to no group (mathematicians' paradox).

Not particularly friendly, this elder man with the trim goatee radiated individuality. That was exemplified by his staunch refusal to ever prescribe damaging psychiatric medications.

His prescription pad might otherwise contain a behavioral prescription ("*Buy her flowers and apologize*") or important notes to himself ("*Fishing with grandson this Saturday: Bring treats*").

Staff usually just left Leon alone. So naturally, we became friends.

I slouched past his office one morning, feeling the weight of my five part time jobs. And the struggles of the patients there at the clinic, plus my own.

Leon yelled: *"Hey Atlas! Put the earth down and rest for a while."*

Strange maybe. But that memory always helped me do just that. Sometimes there *is* a perfect thing to say.

In the 1970s the city was overloaded with special problems, known also as unique individuals. Governor Ronald Reagan had closed major state mental hospitals. They had been unhelpful at best, so good as far as it went. But Reagan failed to pass the financial savings on to us at the community clinics.

Many liberated mental patients expanded the homeless ranks in the streets. Some kept from starving by getting arrested. One tried to take a shower in one of our clinic urinals. Many walking along in busy tourist areas were continuing loud conversations with themselves. (If only we had fake cell phones to give them back then, nobody would have noticed.)

Many of these newly lost on the streets, actively or passively, took the option of leaving their life.

In mornings, the sidewalk in front of a nearby McDonalds was a spot where their remains would be found.

CSP staff were often regarded in more traditional mental health centers as special problems in their own right- creative, effective, famous pioneers, and very hard to categorize.

CSP took on clients the regular centers preferred not to see, even in San Francisco: the newly homeless delusional or suicidal refugees from the defunct mental hospitals, addicts, sexual life style pioneers, and even much sought felons.

And while the five other county centers left their empty offices to do not much more than community outreach, our CSP was the one that still also gave face-to-face psychotherapy to the city's citizens.

Leon's reputation rested more than anything else on his evening *contact groups* with self-selected suicidal walk-ins. A contact group was a gathering of people without cost, record, or paper.

In fact, CSP was proud to be the last such center in the country to give clients the option to be un-digitized.

CSP Director Gene Turrell, formerly with Kinsey's group, specialized in transforming felons wanted by the law, including killers. It was his belief that by doing so in absolute confidence, he was saving more victims. Without that, he was sure, the felons and killers would not be likely to come in.

When law officers sat in his office demanding information on any of these, Gene, a chain smoker, would shut his office door and then fill the room with smoke.

Gene looked like 'Lurch' from the Addams family, wore size 18 shoes.

Law would retreat without what they came for, smoke blown up their visit.

Leon let me sit in one night with his contact group. One of the 13 people there said: *"I have nothing to live for!"* Leon: *"Yes! That's your reason."*

Some were confused, other contact group regulars smiled.

Leon went on to explain that finding your individual purpose in existing on this earth was the most important thing you can do.

"Start looking" he said. Then others reported their progress.

Yes, Leon was very existential in his approach. It worked.

Our staff gathering place was Ernie's, a Chinese restaurant on Polk Street, a block from work. One day I walked in to see something I had never seen before.

Leon sat quietly alone in a corner table with tears streaming down his cheeks.

A waitress we knew whispered: *"His grandson had an accident at school and died yesterday. Very sad."*

Leon's grandson was the happiest part of his days. Whenever he spoke of him, he would transform into smiles. Clearly, his grandson was Leon's purpose in living. And now...

I sat next to Leon. He acknowledged me with a nod but said nothing.

Whatever could I say to this good man that would help him through this trauma?

I could think of nothing.

So I just put my hand on his forearm and sat with him in silence.

Leon eventually pushed his untouched plate of food away.

Quietly said *"Thank you Atlas. I appreciated that."*

He left the restaurant and wasn't seen at work for a few weeks.

When he returned, his contact groups re-commenced.

Leon seemed to have found there another purpose for his existence.

And I had learned this:

When you can think of nothing helpful to say, nothing is what to say.

Enter the Hippo

Themes: *Hit the Road Jack* Ray Charles; *Baby Elephant Walk* Henry Mancini

Many of the staff at San Francisco's Center for Special Problems (CSP) became famous in our field eventually. Back in the 197os it was already apparent.

These included pioneers like lesbian couple Phyllis Lyon & Del Martin, lesbian mother of four (and future Police Commissioner) Pat Norman, bisexuality advocate Maggie Rubenstein, brilliant doctor for pregnant addicts Josette Mondanaro, and a vocal raft of gay male psychiatrists.

In a staff meeting, one social worker complained that the gay psychiatrists did most of the talking, to which one replied *"And rightly so!"*

A social worker named Ron, whose last name I don't recall, was a leader in a successful movement to remove homosexuality as a "disease" diagnosis from the psychiatric DSM manual. I joined in by publishing an article suggesting that if any non-normative sexuality was going to be considered a disease, then celibacy needed to be added and numbered in the DSM diagnostic categories[*].

---

[*] Morgan, R.F. (1975) Revising the Diagnostic & Statistical Manual (DSM-II, DSM-III) of Mental Disorders by adding iatrogenic categories and recognizing celibacy as sexual deviation. *Journal of Irreproducible Results*, 1975, <u>21</u>(2), 31.

Ron's next target to remove stigma from the Gay community was the Vatican. Success? Well, not yet.

While, as a straight white male, I at first seemed not of a good fit within this staff context. But in comparison, I self-identified as an obvious minority with an alternative lifestyle. As such, this straight white male was fully accepted.

It helped that I had brought in a dozen volunteer pre-doctoral psychology interns from my other job as a Dean at the free-standing California School of Professional Psychology.

Even more so for that one day at the motel.

Motel Relief

I was at CSP all day and into the evening one day a week. Besides supervising the interns, I had a very full practice with fascinating clients.

Still, I had fully noticed how very hard everybody else worked.

So one day I rented a room at the motel next door to CSP.

It had a swimming pool. Which allowed me to bring guests. Exercise room. The room was clean, including the bathroom. Everything one would want for a great breakroom.

All day long, staff in small numbers would take breaks in the pool or other motel facilities. Lunch hours were fully used there as well. Often enjoyed by the pool.

Especially since, on the other side of the motel, was a popular inexpensive fast food restaurant with tasty take-outs.

It was called *HIPPO HAMBURGERS*:

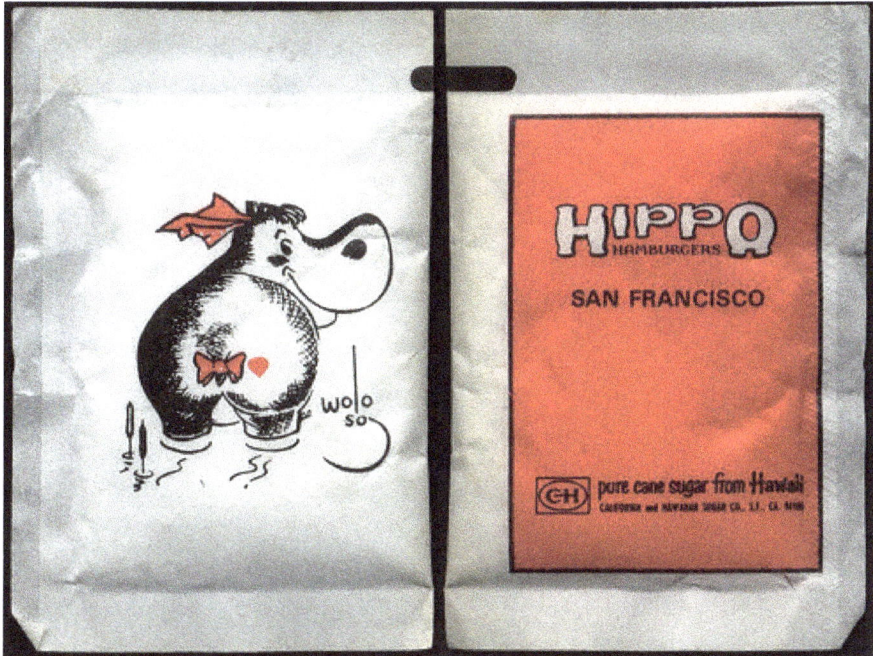

Now it did not go unnoticed with our clinical staff that the hippo image might well be an unflattering portrayal of their fast food customers.

After eating their food there regularly.

Reminds me of another fast food place I took my daughters to.

Until they pointed out that we were eating their happy animal.

It was in the restaurant title as depicted on a large front sign.

And on all their napkins and menus.

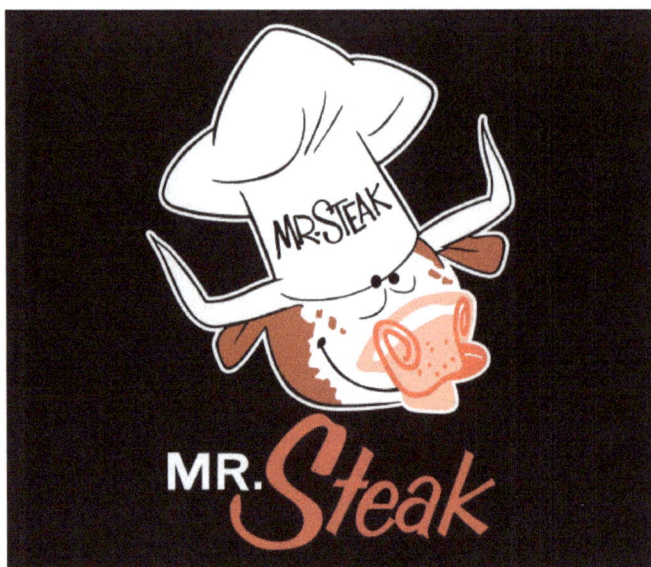

But on that sunny day in San Francisco, the alternative of delicious Hippo burgers banished any such negativity.

On that day.

Addiction Alternative

Our sexual orientation clients were matched in numbers by the addiction-treatment ones. In those days, heroin was the main problem. My dear friend Dr. Josette Mondanaro offered a methadone transition program for pregnant heroin addicts that was successful in its production of healthy non-addicted babies.

Time for me to learn as much as I could about overcoming damaging substance addiction.

I never needed a car in those San Francisco days. Walking usually, buses if needed.

Though if the time and distance were important, cabs were plentiful, inexpensive. That year I had a regular cabbie I could count on, a stocky gravelly-voiced man in his thirties. He knew I was working at CSP.

So one day, he pulled the car over and turned to me. Said he was a heroin addict. He was planning to go 'cold turkey' on his own that weekend. Just stop. He knew that the withdrawal would be rough, to say the least. Wondered if he could call me at home to talk him through it if necessary. No, he would not be a patient at CSP. He had to do it himself. On his days off. Then back to work, clean.

I gave him my home phone number and planned to be there for him that weekend.

First though: *"You can repay me by trying something I just read about. It said that a gram of vitamin C taken every hour with a glass of water may block withdrawal symptoms. Try it?"* He agreed.

That weekend he didn't call the first day. On day two he did. Said he had followed the regime, C every hour with a glass of water. And, amazing, no withdrawal. He skipped the pill and water for two hours. Was on the floor with nausea and pain. Went back to taking C with water every hour, sleeping around this. Peed a lot. Withdrawal ended now he was on the C regime. He would continue.

The last day of the weekend, at night, came his other call. He was clear of heroin now and no withdrawal. He would like to see me for follow up sessions at CSP to make sure it lasts.

What had he learned? He never in his life wanted to see another vitamin C pill.

Addiction Sharing

There is always a risk of doctors becoming infected by their patients. Yes, this can happen psychologically as well as physically.

We become like those we spend our days with. Freud liked to call aspects of this countertransference. "The medical student's disease" describes the feeling that interns often have that the symptoms of a disease they are studying may seem to suddenly appear in themselves.

Some protections can be learned. Should be learned.

Along these lines, I noticed that every week money was collected for staff coffee. The strongest coffee money could buy. Needed! Seemed like an addiction to me.

But first a nod for a tougher habit.

Path Diverted

A non-psychiatric medical doctor joined us. He noted my observation about the staff coffee addiction. But wanted to go for a tougher fight. He, way ahead of his time, wanted to begin a program to help clients stop smoking. Nicotine addiction is even tougher than heroin to beat. Designed that way by cigarette companies.

He knew I didn't smoke. He wanted my help with the success evaluation part. Sure.

I suggested first we invite staff support for the new program. He agreed.

Put together a half-page brief questionnaire for staff. A place to write their specialty.

He balked at the last yes-or-no question I had added: *"Do you believe smoking is bad for your health?"*

He said that for staff in a public health clinic that was insulting. Even in those years, the 1970s, they all knew it was an emphatic yes. But he eventually allowed the question.

All the staff answered the brief survey, 100%.

As to my question, all the psychologists and social workers, community workers, and even the interns said yes. Smoking is harmful to their health.

All the psychiatrists and nurses said no. Most were avid smokers, including the clinic director.

Well, better he should know.

Demoralized, that nice medical doctor transferred out.

Back to the Coffee Addiction

This week it was my turn to collect staff money for the power coffee buy. My name had come up on the alphabetical list. I didn't drink coffee myself (preferred *Oxylent* lemon-flavored vitamin drink to wake up) but soldiered to the task.

Rather than going office door to door, just ran off a note for their mail boxes saying they could each leave their coffee donation in a safe designated space and I will buy the coffee for them when all had complied.

I needed to lighten up the mood as cash requests are never fun, especially the ones that must be paid. So I added a cartoon I'd found at the top of the note.

Recalling our recent motel pool break with Hippo burgers, it was of two standing hippos dancing with each other. Something like this:

 or this

Enter the Hippos

Overall, the staff responded well to the note. I bought their coffee, supported this need. Guilty. But wait.

I was called into the CSP director's office. He said two of the nurses wanted to file charges against me for sexual harassment.

What?

They said the dancing hippos on my note were mocking them. They both were somewhat heavyset. I could see that Director Turrell was trying to take this seriously. We both cared about staff morale.

But he clearly was suppressing a laugh.

I brought it out, saying: *"If the hippo fits."*

He did explain to them that I was referencing a fast food restaurant that we all regularly enjoyed and had never had them in mind.

They reluctantly retreated to their office.

Maybe submerged there.

Meantime most staff office doors had a note taped to them.

Somebody had xeroxed my dancing hippos with a caption below:

HIPPOS SAY FREE DOCTOR MORGAN

Coffee addiction does have a bright side.

The Invisible
Community Worker

Theme: *Searchin'* Coasters

First time on the job but Reggie had from the start been missing for weeks. No message, no response. Then, on payday, he came in, all smiles, to collect his paycheck.

San Francisco 1971

The Center for Special Problems or CSP was one of five city and county mental health centers. Acknowledged as deserving its "Special" title. Some said it was the unique staff, some said it was their Polk Street region sexual lifestyle or addict clients or unfunded street people, not very welcome elsewhere. Most acknowledged though that while the other mental health centers staff were now mostly out in the community, the CSP still welcomed people who could enter the actual building to get their individual or group therapy in person.

But, to be comprehensive, a community work program was added. To lead it, a newly arrived expert from New York was hired to lead it.

Pat Norman

She was already famous. The first lesbian divorced mother to gain sole custody of all four of her children. A leader from the start of the struggle for LGBTQ rights. And there was also that *Doonsbury* cartoon: *"In San Francisco's Board of Supervisors election, running there is a Black woman, an American Indian, a white woman, a community worker, an activist, and a Lesbian mother of four. So what? It's all the same person."*

Pat Norman strode into the CSP, severely beautiful, ready to organize her program then and there. No nonsense.

By the end of the day she had recruited staff, professionals, clients, and street people into an intense two-week training focused on reaching out and uplifting street people. The second week was supervised assistance directly on those very streets.

Ahead of its time by decades, it was possibly the earliest effective initiative for urban homeless people.

At the close of the training she had already chosen her first fulltime employees for the CSP Community Outreach Program.

Reggie was one of them. Black and Gay, he was a street hustler now ready to help.

Reggie

No Reggie on opening day. Pat and CSP staff tried to reach him with no success. No response. Nor any message from Reggie. So no excuse.

Another community worker heard a rumor that he had been seen at a local bar playing pool.

Pat was not pleased. She set aside spending any more time on Reggie until his mystery would be solved. The program roared ahead without him.

Until that first payday.

Reggie was there to collect his check. Smiling.

Pat reminded him she was his supervisor. Where in hell had he been and also- why?

Reggie explained to her and the staff that had gathered to hear this, that

> *"I was out in the community! Being an Outreach worker! How else to do it? Plus I had all your fresh training ready as needed. What's the problem?"*

Pat didn't bother to explain that he was supposed to fit his work into the team as led by his supervisor, her, which involved reporting in and evaluating success as it could be measured, an ongoing revision of action based on daily results.

No. More concise. She fired him. No paycheck.

The Process

But this was a city and county office. There was a process.

Within the hour, CSPO's Director and HR rep had called in all the staff to meet with Pat and Reggie. Pat formally indicated why he had been fired. Never came to work. Unresponsive. Dismissive of any supervision or structure.

Now it was Reggie's turn. He was told he had the option to choose a CSP staff member there at the time to speak for him, present his side.

Reggie looked about the room, considering those of us standing there.

Smiling confidently, he pointed at me. Saying *"I choose him!"*

Surprised, I just said *"Why me?"*

I was a psychologist, not a community worker. An innocent bystander?

Reggie said *"Because you were the only one in this crowd that was smiling at me."*

I had found his blatant no-apologies style amusing. So much for smiling.

How in the world could I defend Reggie's actions though? Pat seemed to me clearly in the right to can him immediately. Well, okay, I stepped up.

The Defense

I was given an hour to consult with Reggie while staff would then reconvene for a final hearing and a vote. HR no longer there as all this process seemed to be the Director's typical way of winging it.

I didn't get much more from Reggie in that time. He did realize he was in trouble, likely to get fired, knew he had ignored the rules. He did want that paycheck and otherwise just wanted to see me justify his office invisibility and dubious (but enjoyable) community outreach. He reassured me that he wouldn't blame me if it went against us.

Damn! He *was* likeable.

I decided to use the time as a psychologist. Got to know him better. Got him to see things from Pat's point of view a disrespectful, nonproductive. Explored what he will do if fired. Useful hour.

All are back now. My turn.

"*Well, Reggie now understands his actions were disrespectful to his supervisor and not helpful to sharing his mission with the team. Nor can he prove that he did any good out there those weeks since evidence of that was not in his mind. He did say it was fun.*" (A few smiles in the audience. Pat not one of them.)

"*Let us take a fresh look from his point of view. Now maybe this was just another hustle on his part. No way to tell. But he has presented us, good or bad, with a different outreach model. He did excel at the Training part, enough to be recruited by his supervisor. What if he really did misunderstand what he was supposed to do once his job began.* (Staff laughter.) *Okay. Not likely. Possible. But he seems too smart for that. O let's just consider his solo model then. An unsupervised rogue approach. Might this be an option for others post-training? To learn what they as individuals can use the training to accomplish on their own. Doesn't work as an employee. Might work as an outcome for trained civilians, Shouldn't some good come from this investment of our time?*"

"*Well, his Solo Community is not what's being considered for a vote now. It's whether Reggie here should be fired as of today. His supervisor has made a compelling case, reasonably, for this. Okay, and we cannot know for sure what was in Reggie's mind during his days of invisibility. Nor does Reggie have his heart set on continuing this job within stricter boundaries, rules, for his behavior.*"

"*So: a misfit for this position? If you think so, realize that even if he is let go as of today, that we might yet send him off with good will and training that may yet do some good. Even for himself as he could now be seen as one of our clients. A paycheck has already been cut and is here. Let's consider it as severance. Please vote on this as well. Thank you.*"

The staff vote was unanimous to exit Reggie (I abstained as did Pat).

The vote was also a bare majority to let him keep his paycheck as severance.

Reggie accepted this with thanks, declined his right to appeal.

Signed up to see me for some individual therapy sessions.

I looked forward to them.

The Schedule

Themes: *Work Song* Oscar Brown Jr/Nina Simone; *Money Honey* Elvis Presley; *Money* Pink Floyd

The 1970s in San Francisco.

By then the Bank of Italy had become the prosperous giant Bank of America. They had issued the first bank credit card, vanguard of the wave of indebtedness we all swim in today.

Their chief financial officer was on the Board of our school of professional psychology. By a fluke, so was I.

Billionaire Norton Simon was on the Board too. He had been directed there by his aged school co-founder and psychoanalyst, Hedda Bolgar of Los Angeles. (She saw patients well past her hundredth birthday in 80 years of practice, though none were seen quite as long as that.) Norton provided half a million dollars of his own money to get the school started. Often joined by his celebrity actress wife, Jennifer Jones.

I had joined a small governing group on this Board to represent the faculty on the San Francisco campus. The Los Angeles campus also had a faculty representative there. And, in the spirit of the times, a graduate student rep from each campus was also there. The four of us were on the Board's executive committee which governed the school along with President Nick Cummings, Treasurer Art Bodin, school Attorney Irwin Leff, and the afore mentioned billionaire philanthropist Norton Simon. From the large Board, President Cummings preferred this small governing group from their number to effectively steer the new school. In directions he preferred.

Art Bodin moved on to further his initiative to found couples and family systems therapy as well as the celebrated think tank Menlo Research Institute (MRI). That left a vacancy for Treasurer which would be determined by our small executive council. At our president's urging, Norton agreed to be treasurer if the group wanted him to do so.

But the student rep from the Los Angeles campus demanded a formal election. President Nick Cummings grudgingly agreed. Nodding reassurance to Norton, he then nominated the billionaire. At which time the student rep nominated me.

I was going to say "*no thanks*" but the president's glare gave me pause.

So why not have a democratic consensus? I agreed to run for treasurer against the billionaire.

Now Norton Simon was affable enough, but he had an automatic attitude of smug comfort that rubbed me the wrong way. He radiated that he owned the earth and could buy anything or anybody he wanted. But in a quiet smiling way.

Probably my own projections at the time. People from Buffalo liked to go overboard at being unimpressed with power.

I didn't need to take the Treasurer spot from him, didn't expect to win. At a young 30, I just wanted to let him know, me smiling quietly now also, that I wasn't intimidated.

The vote was four to three in my favor with the faculty and student reps going my way.

Norton shrugged. Nick seemed torn between rage and tears. Just observing his body language, my impression was reasonably sure that he was appalled. You think?

I thanked them all for their confidence. Suggested each of us immediately donate a mere 1% of our net worth to the school (one dollar for me, somewhat more for Norton). The billionaire declined. Nick the next day expanded the executive committee so the campus reps and I became a minority. He was somewhat mollified when Norton Simon gave a further contribution to the school, seemingly amused by the election. I was reminded that he was a great patron of the arts and museums. Then too, I was the recipient of much support from the faculty and students at both campuses. Many of them surprised by my election, energized by my rudeness.

The 1970s were years of rebellion.

Nick's revenge was to assign me as Treasurer to work with a member of our larger Board, the chief financial officer (CFO) of the Bank of America. The CFO was going to steer us into a new expanded building for the San Francisco Campus. Well, an entire floor in the Bank of America's headquarters building.

I was introduced to him at a reception. My soon-to-be-ex-wife was with me. I had briefed her before she met him that he was in charge of the money of already one of the richest banks in the world.

She radiated intense interest on meeting him. He was impressed. By her.

I was then urged caution by many friends. This banker was said to be notorious for sexual harassment and yet was too wealthy to worry about lawsuits.

And: the next day he invited me to meet with him at his office to go over floor plans and sign papers, adding *"Bring your wife"*.

That next day I was directed to his office on the top floor. On arrival, I admired the view of the city but wondered where his desk was. The room had a spacious double-wide black leather couch, some comfortable chairs, and an especially plush one that he sat in. There was a bar, some edible snacks, a TV, phone. No desk.

He had only two things to say: *"Where's your wife?"* And: *"I don't need a desk. I'm only here for one afternoon a week. That may seem like a pretty short schedule to you, to most people, but in those few hours I make decisions that impact billions of dollars and as many people."*

Clearly allergic to noncompliance, he said the papers weren't ready to sign yet but would be the next day. Even though it wasn't his day to be there. Same time, same place, but *definitely* bring my wife. If I was too busy to be there, I did teach a class then, just send her instead and he would give *her* the leasing papers.

Maybe more, I thought.

The next day I asked a friend to do my class and showed up at the banker's penthouse office at the required time. The lights were low, quiet music coming from somewhere.

I made no excuses for the spousal absence nor did he delay a response. Said he had to cancel and would get back to me.

He called my school's President Cummings minutes after I left, said the lease had fallen through. He had no more time for the school's Board either.

Never saw him again.

I was impressed by his work schedule though.

At a certain level of prosperity, a weekly work schedule can shrink remarkably.

Historically, unions fought for years to reduce the 6.5 day week to the five day 9-5 forty hour work week.

Maybe with automation and AI especially, that work week could be further reduced to possibly three days with full time salaries still intact. Four days per work week are already here. Often in hospital settings now, though at times and in some settings each work day inflates to 10 hours. At the worst end of the spectrum, some settings run M-F **8 to 5** instead of the longtime classic **9 to 5**. Same salary.

Yet, at this writing, the majority of work settings are no longer completely in the office M-F. Remote and hybrid combinations or fewer days per week abide.

More than fifty years later than my visits with the CFO banker at BOA, today's monopolistic private equity owners should feel momentary awe for this predecessor, working *several* hours reliably each week.

Plus maybe a microscopic tear of pity for that particular banker's day of unrequited desire.

The Werewolf

Theme: *Born to be Wild* Steppenwolf

San Francisco State University 1974

Near the end of my class, I took some time to let any student with questions ask them.

It being the 1970s, *any* question would be okay.

A large student with a wild full beard and with long pointed finger nails painted black.

He stood up from the middle of the large group, and let forth: *"Do you believe in werewolves?"*

I responded: *"That hypothesis can be tested. In the night of the next full moon, stand facing it directly. You will have supporting evidence if your facial hair RECEDES."*

He laughed and the class joined in. Teaching the right students can be a lot of fun.

Fun

Themes: *Fun* Sly and the Family Stone; *The Spaghetti Westerns Music* Ennio Morricone; *Juliet of the Spirits* Nino Rota

"Dining at The Old Spaghetti Factory is an experience. For decades we have invested meticulous attention to our unique décor and classical designs. Every location is adorned with antique lighting, intricate stained glass displays, large colorful booths, and an old-fashioned trolley car for guests to dine in. It's the perfect atmosphere for a family celebration."

In San Diego, it was just the three of us. My two young daughters and me. We got there in the summer of 1978.

Back from Australia I was replenishing our funds by working three jobs. Doing outpatient psychotherapy 50 hours a week, 10 hours day, four week days and Saturday. Doing a weekly night supervision seminar for the California School of Professional Psychology's San Diego campus. And then, a full time senior faculty member at San Diego State University went into rehab the first day of his classes, so I took on his full time load of three classes in his place (luckily his seniority meant all three of these classes were on the same day, Thursday, so that filled my fifth weekday).

What about the children? School was not yet open. The older daughter was a very mature ten, the younger at eight matched this, so they both would be safe in the right setting.

Luckily San Diego had one of the best zoos in the world.

And it was surrounded by museums, Balboa Park.

I got them summer passes to all these treats. They would spend my work days exploring. Then we would all be together at the end of the day, before dark, for a meal and recounting of the day's adventures.

Sunday was special though. We would sleep in, then dress up, and convene at a great restaurant together. At first, when funds were low, it was the *Chicken Pie Shoppe*.

Then, we discovered the *Old Spaghetti Factory*. Its theme was "*Fun*". In that specific place, by the door, was a huge stand on digital scale so we could weigh ourselves before and after the meal.

We ate together in a unique and colorful booth.

On a shelf at head level was a dramatic statue of a stallion rearing up on its hind legs.

Once the meal was done, I put a few surviving spaghetti noodles on the horse's back to simulate a saddle. Behind its rear, I placed a small section of napkin with a little meatball on it.

This tableau was greeted with laughter from the children.

Then I left an excessive tip on the table, paid the bill at the register.

We weighed ourselves, and we exited.

The ten year old, once outside, tried out her favorite word of the season.

Her sister was still laughing about my horse's add-ons.

So, of course, the older one said to me *"Why?"*

Why the food on and behind the stallion?

I explained *"To let them know that we had fun."*

1980s
CAUSE AND EFFECT

The busiest day of the year for plumbers is the day after Thanksgiving.

Back to Canada

Theme: *Happy Talk (from "South Pacific")* Rodgers & Hammerstein

Sailors spending much of their lives at sea have developed specialized language, some with obvious origins, some not generally known.

The origin of the "poop deck", for example, needs little explanation. Other terms might.

Nova Scotia Flashback

As has been noted, the 1960s closed with us in the town of Wolfville in western Nova Scotia.

Wolfvillle overlooks the Bay of Fundy.

Looking like a fair-sized lake, the Bay completely disappears daily when pulled by the world's strongest tides into the Atlantic. Its attached streams disappear too then, fish and all.

The Bay remains dry long enough for a picnic where water once was and, soon enough, will come roaring back.

Yes, fish and all.

The highest point overlooking all this is Blomidon Mountain.

Blomidon?

Ever since early sailors sitting in a bar at mountain's edge there viewed the Bay's departure and eventual reappearance, their expression of surprise, *"Blow Me Down"*, stuck with the mountain.

Local dialect, "lawyers pronounced *'liars'* and a garage called a *"gradge"*, may have helped. As did the universal human language desire to shorten and condense words.

Then in the 1980s Ontario

I grew up on the American side of Lake Erie but in summers visited the Canadian Crystal Beach in Ontario. Vinegar on fries instead of ketchup. Fine either way.

When the American dollar was worth more, the sign on Canada's side said *"Welcome Americans"*. When that was not the case, no such sign was to be found.

Still, it seemed to me that in the Canadian bilingual country of both French and English, it was the latter spoken much the same as in our New York state to the south. But like what you put on fries, the differences could surprise you.

I took on a two-year job as a department head at an Ontario university.

My two daughters were middle school age and began day one in what we thought was an English-speaking school. They came home that day discouraged. The problem was not learning French which they did very well. It was the Ontario version of English.

One was laughed at for reading the line *"The sun shone"*. In Ontario it was to be pronounced *"The sun shawn."*

The other found peer turbulence for pronouncing *"schedule"* as *"skedual"* instead of the Canadian *"shedual"*.

She also had to relearn that the alphabet did not end with *Z* pronounced *"Zee"*. No, it was now to be pronounced *"Zed"*.

"I have been" was now to be pronounced as "I have *bean*" and not as in the South of the Canadian border USA style "I have *bin*".

They made the mandated dialect changes in their spoken language. Then did very well as their school days went by.

I was ready for this in teaching my first clinical psychology class. I put the word *"schedule"* on the Board and pronounced it with the American hard k: *"skedual"*.

The class jumped all over this American pronunciation. Clearly explained to me that I was in Canada now and any word beginning with *"sch"* is to be pronounced as *"sh"*. Not '*sk*'.

So, like my daughters, I duly repronounced "schedule" as though it were *"shedual"*.

Okay. Ready now.

I wrote *"Schizophrenia"* on the board.

Asked the class to pronounce it in the correct Canadian way: *"Shitzophrenia"*.

Silence. Laughter.

So easy from that day in the class to better understand and welcome the inconsistencies of diversity in language.

And all else.

The Naked Latvian

Theme: *Might as Well be Spring* Astrud Gilberto

"Results?! Why I have gotten a lot of results. I know several thousand things that won't work."

-Thomas Edison, 1930.

"You can tell a poacher by how he orders his eggs."

–Uncas Slattery, 2000.

We ask psychological tools to guide us in the three aspects of description, prediction, and communication. We ask of evaluation much more. The longer we have been in the field, the more experiences come to mind, a regular historical buffet of past events. Here are a few.

Personnel Selection

While a visiting professor in Canada, I was asked by a local bank president to assist him in a personnel transition situation. I agreed to develop a battery of computer scored tests that might add a dimension of understanding to the administrators being evaluated, but with the caveat that an actually hiring or promotion decision should include a personal interview and actual performance data.

He asked me, as a consultant, to just do a pilot try for him with only the test results. So he submitted the responses of three administrators to me and the computer digested them, regurgitating impressive charts and graphs. I then met with the bank president and his key staff to go over the findings.

I decided to go with the most uncomfortable one first. "This person's results suggest a person who is highly likely to depart from accepted ethical practice and would be a hiring risk" was my kindest interpretation of the sociopathic pattern on the charts. The president grinned widely and everybody looked relieved. "Yes" he said "we had him take this test just before we fired him and had him arrested for embezzlement. I told you this testing was the way to go. Why, look at how much trouble we would have saved if we had known this early on!"

So this was a test of the test. Hmmm. I moved on to the second set of results. "This person is a highly creative and intelligent individual that should be highly successful at whatever he undertakes" I said, hoping it was not another felon. "Right again!" said the president and all grinned, especially the highly successful vice president who had taken the test and was sitting right there in the group.

At that point I had a feeling I should quit while I was ahead (or "Quit while you are behind" as my youngest daughter liked to say). The probability of a third and final success seemed remote, particularly now that it was clear that all three sets of results were already well known employees.

But, following many caveats again, I was ready to move to the last of the three protocols, an apparently straightforward one. "This person is normal in all respects, stable and reliable. His only low scores are in creativity and independent thinking. As long as ideas come from others and the situation is well structured, he would do well, possibly in accounting or maintenance." Following a long silence, the president said "Well, I suppose that is about right. Thank you professor." Of course, the third set of results was from that president. My departure was cordial enough, all things considered. It was Canada after all. I was not invited back.

Preconceptions

While still there in Canada, my colleague Don Marum and I were called in to consult with the regional hospital's psychiatric staff. The affable chief psychiatrist (it happens) took us to the only locked ward.

There were a variety of developmentally disabled adults engaged in various desultory activities. The Chief took us to the far corner where an immense naked man sat, his arms folded and his lips in a pout. He probably held the weight of two men and reminded us of how close we humans are to primates as he sat there in pink skinned obesity and hairy belligerence.

We were told that he was from Latvia and spoke very little English but was assumed to be of very low intelligence. Because of his size, staff was reluctant to force him to keep his clothes on and had turned to us.

Dr. Marum immediately noted that the patient must have a huge appetite. He suggested that he be put on a behavioral reinforcement regime where he would be fed a treat for every article of clothing he put on.

While the Chief was mulling this over, I asked him "Why do you think he doesn't want to put his clothes on?"

Marum and the Chief seemed to think this question was not helpful and ignored it, so I asked a more specific one: "*When* does he put on his clothes?" That was easier to answer: whenever he is allowed out of the locked ward to go on a walk.

Once it was determined that he was no danger to anybody I requested that he be moved to an unlocked ward. Once this was done, the naked Latvian posed no further problems.

The Chief psychiatrist was so pleased with this outcome, he invited me back to see if we might do some evaluation research together. I chose to evaluate their use of electroshock treatment (ECT) and, to my pleasant surprise, he agreed. (This was before we could prove definitively in an evidence based way with MRIs etc. that ECT was such a high risk procedure that it should never be used).

As to measures, he wanted ward behavior compliance and I wanted measures of cognitive function and brain damage. Despite our different expectations and interests, we did agree in the end to use all the measures we each wanted.

And then came the research design. I wanted him to randomly choose half those who were going to get ECT and withhold it from them so we might have a control group. He vetoed that approach, saying withholding treatment would not be ethical, and wanted to assign ECT to a random group of patients who would not ordinarily get it. This I vetoed.

Clearly our expectations of what this invasive treatment would or would not do, prohibited any research. It would take modern MRIs and CAT scans to prove the issue of damage, although it still remains a psychiatric tool despite the proof.

Our ECT research was never done at that hospital but we did make a naked Latvian happier.

Validity

First I have learned to agree on the *purpose* of assessment, such as the *question* to be answered or the *mission* to be achieved. Then use the measure most likely to yield clear data that can be usefully interpreted.

All else is inductive from there.

Student feedback on the effectiveness of their instruction and instructor is often littered with 10 point scales and hard to interpret questions.

One might think this was a deliberate way to obfuscate the results, particularly from administrators trying to quantify impact on ordinal scales.

A simple % satisfaction score is probably the most interpretable. I also very much lean toward dichotomous choices if it is a dichotomous question and, in general, brief and concise measures. The 12 point scale may *look* more valid but if it is truly a yes or no question, what in the world will three decimal points add?

Nor do the number of pages in a psychological test add to any genuine validity.

Exceptional Measures

Some test items seem somewhat strange but I suppose if the numbers show reliability and validity, being counter-intuitive is fine.

I am waiting though for items like: *"Sometimes I feel like none of the questions on this test have anything to do with me."* or *"When sweets are served do you feel lonely and desserted?"*

We also know that time is an important variable in testing (Morgan, 2004b). It used to be assumed, for example, that the older adults get, the lower their tested intelligence. Even before the contemporary differentiation of fluid and crystallized intelligence, Nancy Woodruff demonstrated that removing the stopwatch from the intelligence testing procedure allowed IQ scores to increase with age rather than decrease. As we get older we get smarter but slower.

Albert Ellis (1984) told me once that he would like every journal article that is published to be followed immediately by a rebuttal. He felt this would lead to a better evaluation of everything. Or, at the very least, a good argument.

I am tempted to include here some of the more interesting applications seen along the path, such as a brief non-invasive standardized test of human aging, efficiency percentages as ways to clarify assessment impact beyond statistical significance, the most powerful genetic assessment technique to get at the roots of gender differences, and an overlooked central tendency method for test item analysis.

Evaluation remains the bedrock for organizational and administrative change and has brought about the empowerment and enhanced effectiveness of many an institution. Now, the most powerful assessment study I can recall was that of the more than 3000 children deprived of public education in Virginia. Our finding, above and beyond critical periods of learning, was that tested intelligence *depends* on education; it varies with the quality of the learning environment. The implications of this study impacted many countries even to this day- Bermuda comes to mind.

My favorite offbeat assessment measure for psychologists was done by California psychologist S. Don Schultz when he held responsibility for the California State psychology license exams. It was before the current national exam. California back then elected to score an essay exam. A major question on the essay exam, Don's favorite, asked us test takers to discuss Public Law 379 as it applied to child custody determination. There *was* no Public Law 379 on child custody determination. The correct answer was *"There is no such law."* An acceptable answer was *"I don't know"* or *"I am not familiar with this law but in other states ..."* A failing answer was to discuss it knowledgeably as though it really existed, to fake it. This item reliably failed the few psychologists taking this test that should never practice.

I got the right answer and Don later told me he knew which paper was mine when he corrected them even though our names had morphed into numbers for the correctors. *"How did you know?"* I asked. *"When you answered the question on how to deal with an invasive government form threatening your client's well-being and privacy by writing 'Answer abusive bureaucratic forms with bureaucratic forms of your own: send them an extensive form to fill out to justify their request', I knew it was you."* Informal days, those.

Observation versus Perception

Lightner Witmer, considered the founder of applied clinical and professional psychology, ran afoul of American professor William James, considered a co-founder of all psychology in parallel timewise with European professor Wilhem Wundt. The issue was assessment. James considered assessment as a form of research. So from that perspective, norms are meaningless unless procedure is held constant. Witmer preferred to follow Galton's path and vary his techniques assessing children based on individual differences, a dichotomy still at times separating researchers from practitioners.

In other words, procedures were flexible depending on the child's needs.

I advocated following James when collecting data and Witmer after the data are collected.

Since most intelligence tests end on cumulative failure, I usually continue with children on easier items long after those data are in so as to make the whole testing experience much less aversive. They end the experience with getting answers right, not on ending in failure.

Also in that era, we have Joseph Bell mentoring Arthur Conan Doyle when Doyle was a medical student and Bell was the Royal Surgeon. Bell's highly perceptive attention to detail and mannerisms have been considered the model for Doyle's eventual Sherlock Holmes novels. One medical demonstration attributed to Bell and passed down through medical school classes for generations was as follows: *Bell marched into the lab followed by a flock of medical residents. He turned to them and said "Diagnosis uses all your senses, Ignore any at your peril. And do not shy away from what must be done for full perception. Here is a beaker of the urine of a patient with a very specific ailment. Let us test your perception and your courage." With that, Dr. Bell dipped his finger into the urine saying "I will now taste my finger for clues. Then it is your turn." One at a time each intern dipped their finger into the urine and tasted it. When all were done, Bell said: "If any of you had watched carefully, you would have noted that the finger I put in the urine was not the finger I put in my mouth. Do not just observe: perceive."*

Here is a more recent Sherlock Holmes story:

"Sherlock Holmes and Doctor Watson went on a camping trip. After a good meal and a bottle of wine, they fell into a deep sleep. Some hours into the night Holmes awoke and nudged his faithful friend. 'Watson, look up and tell me what you see.' Watson replied 'I see millions and millions of stars.' 'What does that tell you?' inquired Holmes. Watson pondered a moment. 'Astronomically, it tells me that there are millions of galaxies and potentially billions of planets. Astrologically, I observe that Saturn is in Leo. Horologically, I deduce that the time is approximately a quarter past three. Theologically, I can see that God is all-powerful while we are but small and insignificant. Meteorologically, I suspect that we will have a beautiful day tomorrow. What does it tell you?' Holmes held his silence for a moment, then spoke: 'Watson you idiot! Someone has stolen our tent!' "

Father's Day

Themes: *Perfect Angel* Minnie Riperton

I was raising two daughters as a single parent. Both were talented and loving.

When they were in middle school, they both competed in a Father's Day Contest. The prize was a $100 savings bond. The challenge was to write the best tribute to Dad in 25 words or less. This was a huge sum for children of that age in those days. So many competed.

My older daughter wrote some beautiful words. They meant a lot to me when she shared them. Even though they didn't win. The younger one submitted a few entries. She enjoyed writing and there was no limit on tries. One that she submitted won the contest:

> *"My father never spanks us. He just gives us a disappointing talk."*

She received the savings bond in a well-attended ceremony.

The MC gave her a big condescending smile and said: *"Little girl. Didn't you mean to say 'disappointed'?"*

She smiled back at him. *"No. I meant disappointing."*

Hap-pee Father's Day

You're the world's greatest dad although my frame of reference is limited.

someecards

One of my college roommates was from Bermuda. He told me that Bermudian males often had children from all over the island. He said that their favorite two things were food and sex. Not in that order.

On Father's Day they hoped to get enough gifts to help with all the presents they needed to deliver all over the island on Christmas. Santas incarnate roamed the island that morning. How many men everywhere else never really know how many children might honestly call them "father"?

Just wait to see who sends them a card on Father's Day?

MOTHER'S DAY

On that day she is clear about this to her children. Covering her lap with both hands: *"You're not ever coming back there!"*

Lilly Tomlin was asked once if she had any children. She responded: *"None that I KNOW of."*

CHILDREN'S DAY

As a child I asked why there wasn't one. The parental answer was always a tired *"That's every day!"*

CONCEPTION DAY

I used to suggest to my class that they find the day and date nine months before they were born and then ask their parents exactly what they were doing on that day. A great discussion gift for both Mother's and Father's Day. Or anytime.

Life Transition Specialists

Theme: *Where's the Money?* Dan Hicks

Fresno 1983. Night had come and only dim light from street lamps came with it. I sat on a downtown park bench thinking about that strange day. The bench was surrounded by thick grass in a mini-park facing our office building. It seemed to me that the grass was moving. Rippling really, like green ocean waves. But no wind that quiet night. No traffic, no noise. Just grass bending in rhythm. Illusion? Look closer. Oh! The grass was being bent by the passage of roaches, armies of roaches. Dark living waves of cockroaches. I moved on.

That summer we opened our private practice. Part time as the three of us worked full time at a free-standing professional school for psychologists. I was the Dean there and my two partners were faculty. Let's call them Len and Bill, much as their parents had named them.

A prevalent psychological problem for regular folks in that community was the stress from some transition. Deaths, divorce, lost jobs, even being new in town. Temporary but intense, caught early before PTSD, these were issues we felt we could contribute to resolving. And, of course, much less stress for clinical psychologists used to more dire and challenging cases.

So we called our practice *"Life Transition Specialists"*. Put that on our business cards- wood grain stock with natural patterns such that no card's patterns were the same as any other.

We found a very inexpensive third floor office in the center of the town, facing a small park. The building was full of other businesses, as I recall, about five floors of them.

Our suite had three offices and a large entry way. Two of the offices looked out on the park. The third was smaller and had no windows.

I only expected to be there part-time since I still had a fulltime job to do, so I took the small office. Bill and Len each loved the space and natural light in their new domain.

Len had an added special skill in hypnosis, Bill in neuropsychology and sexology. They were confident, skilled, used to being seen as handsome. We were single and in our early forties. What could go wrong?

We were licensed for private practice and ready to go. As soon as the **LIFE TRANSITION SPECIALISTS** sign was up and we were moved in, we knew our presence had to be announced. Since we still lacked patients.

We decided to begin with the businesses in our own office building. We would have an Open House. The date was set, the announcement delivered to every office in the building. The door to the suite was opened at 4 PM that day, refreshments in the open space, all office doors open. The two large offices helped light up the suite with the natural afternoon sunlight through their windows. Very inviting.

We were first visited by a few young and attractive secretaries from varying offices. One visiting me, sat in my office and shared this insight: *"We thought from your business name that you were morticians"*.

Maybe we should have called it Life *Crisis* Specialists.

She went on that none of them were there for therapy, just to check out the eligible males. Consenting adult prospectors.

Len overheard this and came by. Offered her a tour of his office. They left together. The natural light dimmed somewhat as Len's office door closed. Soon followed by audible grunts of passing pleasure. For quite a while.

The natural light dimmed further and was gone. Bill's door was closed now too. His girlfriend was visiting and being treated to a tour of her own. Clearly this second job was seen as mainly recreational by my partners.

My office was the only one open, so I hosted new visitors as they came. If I had followed the examples of my partners, the Open House would have been over before it really started. Still, nobody was hurt. And several were very pleased by our most obliging hosts. Our ethics were intact. The visiting secretaries were neither patients nor students.

As it was, my small office and dim office lighting were far from impressive. Though the refreshments were consumed and visitor curiosity satisfied. One late visiting secretary was really disappointed as she had lost a parent recently and had hoped to make final arrangements for the remains (a term not to be used when clearing the table at Thanksgiving).

When the day was done, we had acquired no patients. I knew that for a while, a few people might be helped by my talented but distracted partners.

And so it would be.

But not for very long.

I came back that evening to sit in the park facing our building. Considering the apparent transition of the life of our own new practice.

Soon I was watching the armies of downtown roaches making night waves, surfing in the thick green grass.

And laughed.

I found the day to have been hilarious.

A Next Generation Hope

Theme: *A Change is Gonna Come* Sam Cooke

Well, that would be a change. Our children would seem to be inheriting a world in its final days. Planet heating toward extinction, war growing ever more lethal, even nuclear soon. Pandemics spreading. Dictatorships multiplying, democracies diminished, division ballooning.

You know the list.

At the time of this writing, maybe all those now militarily acknowledged UFOs, from the future, deepest ocean, or elsewhere, are all just here to witness this dramatic extinction.

So how about some light on the remote possibility that the human family can somehow unify at this last moment and surmount these threats. Open a path to a better future. Survive.

There is a memory that might on a very small scale predict such a possibility.

Fresno, California, in the 1980s

Fresno is next to some great national parks and some high polluting billion dollar agriculture.

The huge rural region around Fresno was then a magnet for Vietnam resettlement refugees and a continuing migration of interracial workers from Mexico and points farther south.

One of my graduate students, Bradford Chang, was doing his doctoral dissertation with me at a professional psychology school there. It was on what psychology can contribute to special education for students in diverse cultures. As part of this work, he was doing his internship in a nearby rural Head Start drawing migrant children from these cultures.

He asked me to join him there and help where I could. I agreed.

Brad worked, quite skillfully, with the children. I found a role by meeting every week with their parents.

To do this, I received the help of four translators. Spanish of course. Also Vietnamese, Laotian, and Hmong.

The parents often began with seeking advice for their Head Start child but, as most had large families, questions soon refocused on the other children. On calls for help to parents dealing with their child's behavioral issues.

I brought in aspects they might not have received from other places.

Based on David Cheek's hypnosis work, I suggested that at the end of each day the parents quietly stop in the sleeping child's bedroom, sit, and gently thank them for anything helpful; or successful that they might have done that day, even by mistake. No complaints though. Just the positive.

I was given some authority here as a credentialed professor, which in these cultures mattered much more than we were used to. So they tried it out and it worked. The behaviors improved.

As the weeks went by, I noticed that the Laotian translator took much longer than the others. It became increasingly clear that he was adding his own improvisations.

A parent who was bilingual met with me and the Laotian translator to sort it out. Mostly the translator's improvisations were reasonable and we soon precluded any more of what wasn't.

The Hmong questions soon moved from children to daily life. These had been mountain people living in basic rugged conditions. Now living in California they had need to sort out the use of a bathtub with a faucet providing running water. I thought it creative when they filled the tub with soil and planted crops that could be irrigated from the faucet. Some other more experience parents clarified the usual alternative option.

From the start, the parents sat in five different clusters. Little or no friendship occurred between clusters. Even some near hostility between a few.

I was often busy trying to have a more unified parent group but no luck.

The North Vietnamese and the South Vietnamese were particularly antagonistic to each other and sat in opposite corners of the room.

The Laotian parents formed their own closed group, discussing their own children's progress.

The Spanish-speaking parents too stayed focused only on their own children's issues, not much on other culture's parents whose languages made communication out of reach.

All seemed to look down on the Hmong and ignored these parents though I found the Hmong to be the most effective at using whatever I suggested. Or, for that matter, what the other Hmong parents had found to work. The Hmong parent group was best at growing as a mutual helper group, one that would continue long after Head Start ended. An important goal.

Brad meanwhile had worked very well with the Head Start staff and children. Tests showed enhanced intelligence, improved educational skills, learned content, and enhanced emotional well-being.

In our supervision sessions, he shared an important observation. None of the children were clustered like their parents. The budding friendships crossed all cultural lines. By the end of the Head Start experience, they all seemed happy, friendly, cooperative, and ready for public school next year.

At my last session with the parents, I shared this information. They all seemed pleased with the success of their children. But I decided to ask.

Why were they still so divided against the other cultures in the room when their own children, at such a young age, succeeded at group unity?

Each of the translators explained this to me until all parent cultures were represented. For once there was agreement.

This was not their original country. They had no interest in making peace outside their own. They saw themselves as fully formed, either with no interest or no ability to change much. Though they would try, they thought they were too old to adapt more than they had to. (Wrong.)

But they had learned here that the main job of a child was to learn how to survive where they were. They were in California now. A very new home.

The children were acknowledged as being at an age where they would be best at adapting. Being unified across cultures was what was done here.

So be it.

The parents saw their children as the future of their family. Each parent said they fully supported friendships and play dates across culture. For their children.

Not for themselves.

They now knew the next generation would survive then.

Their children would adapt as survivors always did.

It was now expected.

Brad became Dr. Chang in 1989.

Aptitude of the Apt

Theme: *Another Brick in the Wall* Pink Floyd

I was Dean of a California campus that was recruiting doctoral students for their clinical psychology program. A national debate was going on as to the value of aptitude tests as a selection device. We, the faculty and me, were arguing about this as well.

The main issue for us at that time was the Graduate Record Exam or GRE. Applicants to a lot of prestigious universities were required to take and submit both the general exam and the specific one on the content of the discipline.

The proponents for GRE argued that the test was established, saved screening time if you just accepted the high end of the scores, and guaranteed them the smartest new students.

The opponents argued that the validity of both subtests was very poor as reflected in studies predicting subsequent grades or post-grad success. It seemed biased against racial or economic minorities, and the specific test had nothing to do with clinical psychology, just general informational knowledge.

The faculty was leaning toward requiring the GRE whether it was valid or not. Going by test scores would save them time and add prestige to the school. The smartest and most talented applicants should still be able to hit the highest scores, if their general knowledge was good enough. Opponents said that was just a test of their prior education which was what gave an advantage to the wealthier applicants. Doing the extra work of interviews and reading the written applications was both fair and worthwhile.

I could count the coming votes in my mind and see that GRE would win by a small margin. So I spoke up: *"If we do decide to require these GRE tests for applicants, fair or not, it makes sense to me that we all take the tests first ourselves. That way we will know by our own experience what we are requiring. Assuming we each do well."*

Ron Gandolfo, a most respected faculty member, stood up to respond: *"Robert! That is the worst idea you have ever had!"*

The unanimous vote was not to require the GRE.

A Language Malfunction

Theme: *Just a Little Rain* Joan Baez; *Stairway to Heaven* Led Zeppelin

"I am SO worried for you! I not want my husband to kill you!"

I was on the boarding line for my plane. She grabbed my arm.

San Francisco psychologist and actor Benjamin Tong gave me many valuable insights on language. One of my favorites was the delicate way in which reviewing an unpleasantly jarring performance might be politely expressed: *"It had its moments"*.

This was one of those moments.

I met her at an international psychology congress, one in my final years of unmarried life. She was from an Asian country that the two formal languages of our association, English and French, were rarely spoken or understood by most of its inhabitants. Nor did the ones I met feel they were missing anything.

Not her though. She struggled to master fairly competent English conversation, possibly overestimating her success. But I admired her effort. Besides, other than a few words learned from movies, I had no command whatsoever of her language.

Her goal was to get an advanced psychology degree, the doctorate.

I doubted her language progress would be equal to the reading or lecture of any graduate program in the English language.

Still, that was exactly what she wanted to do. With my guidance.

I was impressed by her as a person. She had wit, poise, beauty, intelligence. Plus the confidence of somebody with near infinite resources.

I told her what I could of seeking the path she wanted to be on. Including acquiring more language proficiency for that choice.

She sat next to me when I saw her again two years later. The international congress this time was hosted in Japan, her own country. This was the Opening Ceremony.

Like the Olympics, countries vied to host these international meetings. For participants in her country, this would likely be the only conference of its kind in their lifetime. As such it was spectacular.

Through her eyes, it represented her own lifelong cultural perspective. The entire event took on unforgettable fresh color and intensity. Full of meaning that, without her, I might have missed completely. This was overall the best Opening Ceremony I had ever seen.

After the ceremony, over dinner, she shared her life story.

Married young to the globe trotting son of the founder of a powerful international company, she was often alone in their home.

She spent each day writing him a letter about her own observations, ideas, and experiences.

At the end of that first year, he published her letters as a book. One that was very well received.

As years went by, the annual book of her comments on that year become evermore popular. She became a celebrity in her own country.

Although no translations to other languages made the books available elsewhere.

Still, each year loyal readers looked forward to tales of this celebrity couple, both traveling now but rarely together.

In fact, this very conference, even our dinner together, might appear in her next book.

Although I would not be able to read it without a translator, I was promised a copy.

We did not meet again after that evening until another international congress four years later.

Once again we sat together at an Opening Ceremony in another country she knew very well.

Just before this conference, she had flown all the way from her own country to Los Angeles just to have lunch at a top restaurant with my youngest daughter, a theater student at UCLA.

She asked my daughter to tell me that she would be at the next World Congress and hoped I could meet her there.

I had already intended to go. So I did.

Now, as we sat through the opening music, tears began streaming down her cheeks. I asked her what was wrong.

She responded with *"My husband and I. We now separated."*

How sad. Her entire public face at her home has been invested in this marriage.

Mortality statistics suggest that a divorce from a longtime part- ner can be more stressful than losing one through death. Worse yet, for such a highly visible couple, to be entering a divorce through the door of a legal separation. And she definitely appeared devastated.

I was not married yet that year. So I spent the next week with her, resolved to cheer her up. We toured the host country together. A very intense and satisfying set of days. Happy statues in time.

Her tears were gone now. She thanked me for her better sleep at night. She promised that now we were a couple, our time together would be highlighted in her next annual book, a central chapter. Untranslated though. Not sure I wanted that particularly. But her gift to me made her happy.

By our last day together, she had become extremely anxious. But she would not say why. Finally, it was time for me to go to the airport. She came along to say goodbye.

As I stood in the boarding line, that was when she told me: *""I am SO worried for you! I not want my husband to kill you!"*

I asked her why she thought that.

Weren't she and her husband separated?

"Yes. It is as I said. Separated. He in London. Me here with you."

—

Note: The next year I met and then married the woman I have been with all these decades.

My billionaire separated friend sent us a $5 cashier's check as a wedding present.

It was not meant kindly of course but we cashed it anyway.

She did send the book detailing our adventure together.

Someday I mean to have it translated.

Higher Ground

Themes: *The Good, the Bad, and the Ugly* Danish National Symphony Orchestra; *Blood on the Saddle* Country Bear Jamboree & Tex Ritter; *No More Drama* Mary J. Blige, *Higher Ground* Stevie Wonder

> *"So profound it is*
> *It dwells within our nature*
> *In all of life's gifts*
> *It is not how much you know*
> *But in what you understand"*

–Kenichi K. Yabusaki
"During the Pause: A Collection of Tanka Poems"
(2022, 2024)

The years 1986-1991. Palo Alto, California

The President

In character, he might well have anticipated the less educated 21st century TV actor leading the *"Make America Great Again"* cult. Or maybe he was already a reincarnation of the 19th century P.T. Barnum. For me, he was the president of a 20th century Palo Alto graduate school. And, as I was his vice president, he was my boss for the last four years of the 1980s.

He was also a fulltime Dean at another university plus running a private consulting business. He also somewhat organized many of the region's other CEOs, seeing himself as the president of presidents. And, unexpectedly, he would take courageous and even brilliant initiatives.

So: busy.

This defined my mission- run the graduate school, excluding his executive office, and get national accreditation from the American Psychological Association. Which I did. In this, I had much autonomy.

As said, he was busy.

The Stock Market Plunge

It was temporary and short of a depression, but one day his stocks took a beating. At first he indulged his legendary bad temper, which mainly hit his kind and patient elderly secretary. He was hard on any that he supervised directly.

Then he called an emergency Board Meeting. These included wealthy CEOs, investors, or their top lawyers. After the meeting, he visited me with a huge smile. Explained it.

He had told them all that our school needed to show support from its Board. Brought out his checkbook and made it out to the school for many thousands of dollars. Passed the check around the table so all could see it. Then challenged each one to match it or better. They had obliged.

I knew this was money he would control, but still asked how he could afford to write a check like that at a time when so much of his stock assets had cratered. He had been waiting for that question. Said he had just approve a salary boost for himself that matched his check *and* exceeded all his stock losses.

Not long after, I wouldn't approve his raiding my faculty budget and that stuck.

The Race

The president was in his 60s and enjoyed being seen as an athlete. Lately this manifested with his weekly runs, highly publicized, running garb, photos, media. He shared with me that he was still being underestimated, probably being at Olympic competition level. Asked me if I ever at least did jogging. Not really, I told him. He thought I was too sedentary for a man twenty years younger. I didn't dissuade him. He enjoyed the comparison.

Truth was I didn't jog because whenever I felt like running, I ran full out like a wild horse. I understood why this felt like freedom for the horses. Me too. Plus, not bothering to own a car, I walked everywhere, probably in the best shape of my life.

The president chose to take me along to an important community meeting. We parked at the back end of the parking lot, maybe a hundred yards from the building front door. When we got out of the car, he looked at his watch and said *"Look Robert, we're running late. So I'm going to use my speed to get there faster. I can't let you hold me back. I will be at the first conference room opposite the third floor elevator. Meet me there whenever you can catch up."*

I nodded. He assumed a racing position and took off. I gave him a few seconds head start.

Then I waited for him to catch up to me at the building's front door.

Substitutions

He often was expected to do things he would rather not do. In these cases, he would choose to have me take his place. I would usually accept since it provided unexpected opportunity.

HP

I recall what happened when we moved the school into some vacant buildings from Hewlett Packard (HP). A Board member was HP's top lawyer.

The best office was set aside for our president. It was on the first floor but elevated so as to give a great view through this bay window of the outside road and all the great scenery beyond it. The building had been the HP security headquarters so that may be why the Bay window had a bullet hole in it, apparently fired from a passing car on the street. Directly opposite the desk where he would be sitting. Noticing this, the president insisted that I take his office while he would take mine, by the faculty. I agreed, moved in.

A month later he came to me for a consultation. Why? HP's lawyer and top Board member wanted to donate their impressive wall-to-wall computer bank to the school. HP had bought newer computers. I asked the obvious questions, Even then, smaller portable computers were replacing the monster ones with no less power. So what would it cost to maintain these donated computers? Too much. Would we need to hire staff to care for and work it? Yes. Do we have an extra room to house it? No.

So why ask me?

Oh. He wanted me to be the one to turn down the HP lawyer's gift. Fine.

The Debate

Another dilemma emerged for the president when two key dignitaries from Stanford University pushed on opposite sides of an argument.

The first was a Board member who was also a distinguished social psychologist. We'll call him "Phil" much as his parents had. He had spearheaded a motion to fund a scholarship for an HIV-positive psychology doctoral student. And he had already endorsed one of his eligible students as the first recipient.

The second was a Stanford physician who was also our Faculty Dean. We'll call him "Dick" as everybody else did. Not in a pejorative sense. I think. Dick opposed the launching of this scholarship opportunity. The Admissions Officer of our school agreed with hm.

Not wanting to be on either side visibly, the president privately always sided with the Board. But if bad news was to be delivered, well, he put me in charge. Said I was to run a debate on the issue while key Board members watched. Students and faculty came too.

AIDs at the end of the 1980s was typically considered an epidemic death sentence. HIV-positive a deadly diagnosis. Phil's student was HIV-positive. Also very bright and talented. Wanted that doctorate so he could provide clinical support to others facing the same life-threating trauma.

So I set up the public debate. Dick and the Admissions Officer would speak first with their objections. On the other side, the president had insisted that Phil *and* the actual student in question would present their side. Seemed kind of unfair for the con side of this argument to tell the student to his face why he should not be brought in. But Dick agreed and it was on. My role was to moderate and make final remarks.

It began. Large crowd.

Dick said, as a physician, that *"the trajectory of life for this student would be very short, only five years at most. Not much time at all to have a clinical practice after finishing a doctoral program."*

The Admissions Officer said that she was concerned about possible drops in applications if the school were seen as a concentration of infected AIDs students.

Next Phil spoke briefly about why his talented student should have this scholarship. Said nothing about AIDs. Just that his student merited the opportunity.

The student was also very brief. Maintaining his composure, he only restated his goal to support others in his position through their trauma.

My turn.

I addressed Dick's concern first. We are all of us on a 'trajectory' in our finite lifespan. Barring a cure, we still cannot refuse a student this opportunity because the time for the practice may be short. We have accepted one student in her 60s and a man who was 72. In addition, the strength involved in fulfilling work likely is in itself a life-extender. Meaning that the opportunity to be a clinical psychologist regularly enhancing the lives of clients facing the same challenges can be healthy for the student. A treatment as powerful as any drug. Finally, he is addressing the needs of a profoundly underserved group. Important.

For the Admissions Officer, I agreed with her. Yes, some applicants, unaware that you can't catch AIDs from sitting in a classroom, may not apply. But others, impressed by this initiative, may be more likely to apply. We really should want more of these and less of the uninformed frightened ones.

I thanked the student for his courage in coming forward and participating. Clarified that his merit was not in question. Thanked Phil for his initiative. (When Phil years later become a President of the American Psychological Association, his theme was *"Giving Psychology Away"* or contributing to our daily life.)

The Board voted as the president wanted. The scholarship was approved and the student accepted.

But the president may have been more impressed with what Dick and the Admissions Officer had said than I was. He also mandated that the student get no shortcuts and must finish all the requirements that everybody else had.

That was not what the student had been promised. He had been told his past courses would transfer and that he could fast track to the doctorate. Save years of which he may have had few.

So he withdrew, choosing instead to have a clinical practice at the Master's level, a degree he already had. I supported him to do so. And that's what he did.

In this way, in the end, the president had satisfied both Stanford factions as well as his Admissions Officer. Not sure what happened to the HIV-positive scholarship program.

The students and faculty that had witnessed the debate were very happy with how the issues had emerged. Especially the gay students who did become a growing and key student force.

As for me, I moved on to the next day.

The Shadow

The Board had gifted him with a reservation to shadow a key California politician. This meant spending a regular work day with him as a silent "shadow" so as to observe this leadership model in action. Being silent was not the president's desire or strength, so I agreed to take his place.

The object of my shadowing was John Vasconcellos of the California Legislature in Sacramento. John was the second most powerful leader there, after Speaker Willie Brown. I knew the Speaker, eventually awarding him an honorary doctorate, in which he proclaimed he now had to be called "Doctor Brown" and would be able to practice psychotherapy. This was his abundant sense of humor which didn't dissuade the legislators of both political parties to respect him as the best leader they ever had or would have. Today, now, he is mainly known as San Francisco's best mayor. But John was new to me.

I saw him use great oratory in debate, courage and conviction in whatever he did that day. I also was there sitting quietly when a man came by to ask John's permission and blessing to run for office in a district. He all but kissed John's ring. Interesting.

During a lull, I noticed that John had a few books readily available on a shelf by his desk. I was pleased to see that one of them was mine. Broke the silence by saying that. John was clearly surprised to be reminded that I was there. Asked which book? I told him it was *The Iatrogenics Handbook,* focused on medical mistakes and their prevention, the third leading cause of death for patients.

That led to a friendship I still remember with respect. John had been the chauffeur for past Governor Pat Brown and worked his way up from there. Eventually he retired and settled in Hawaii. In time he returned to Santa Clara, dying there in 2004.

The Quintet

By my third year, we had earned our accreditation and the school was doing very well. I had been able to access the Bay Area's deep bench of talent, hiring many outstanding faculty and recruiting wonderful graduate students, diverse and brilliant. Easy to treat them with the respect and justice they deserved.

My initiative to affiliate with Stanford University had come through. Their accreditation had been granted for their clinical psychology doctoral program, based likely on Stanford's high world status, even though they had only three faculty to run it, and one of them was the dean. So they diverted their students through our graduate school for their key courses. The president by then was hinting that it might be nice for me to take a job as president of my own university. Meaning move on soon.

Then the Board once again gave him a gift reservation, this time for a very expensive leadership skills upgrade program designed for CEOs. The president was convinced his leadership skills needed no brushing up. But believing the gift must be accepted and fulfilled, he sent me in his place. I had been intrigued and went.

There were 25 of us, mostly top administrators of Bay Area companies. I felt out of place with these profit-oriented folks but blended as best I could. We had a whole day to go.

At first we were asked to, one at a time, announce our first name, our title, and something about ourselves. People there were to raise their hands in any order when they were ready. I felt ambivalent. Go first, last, or in the middle?

Once we were done, it took a while, we were treated to a video filmed of us during that exercise. As it ran silently, the trainers wanted any of us that had learned something about themselves from the video to share it. I went first this time.

My hand raising showed my ambivalence. It was only half up and moved around vertically. Made me look indecisive, weak. A carryover from grade school? I thought of myself as decisive but this projected the opposite. My hand should go up with conviction when I was ready. As from that time, it will. The trainers liked this and the flow from others on their own learning was useful.

After a few other planned lectures and training exercises, we came to the grand finale. We were told to divide into five groups with five trainees in each. Our choice where in the large room to meet and what group to be in. But make it fast.

More decisive this time, I went to a corner of the room and waited for four more to join me. One woman and three men did so. One of the men carried himself like my home president. He clearly expected to be our leader. The other three looked worried, looked to him and me. The four other groups had formed at the other room corners, with one in the room's middle. The trainers distributed to each of us a copy of a ten line commercial for an imaginary product. Each group was going to be allotted three minutes to present the copy. The best group presentation would be decided by a vote from all the trainees. We would now be given five minutes to decide what to do.

The trainers finally told us to pick a spokesperson to lead our group. I nominated the one who seemed to need that. The other three, seeming relieved, agreed. He was surprised. Whispered to me *"Thanks, I think. But I don't know what to do."* I whispered back *"Just direct me to come up with a plan. Be decisive."*

This he did.

I had the group members each agree to read two lines. Be creative. Once these were sorted in order, our leader first, I told them we would spread out over the front of the room, an arm's length from each other. I asked our leader to announce our groups name at the beginning of his lines. Name? There would be five of us. How about *"The Quintet"*? OK. Oh and we would wait and go last.

The groups were told to come up in any order they chose. Now with all trying to be decisive, there was no hesitation. One after another, five trainees would go to the front of the room and their spokesperson would alone read the copy, varying in style, volume, emphasis, charisma, and then sit down.

Our turn. We shared the lines equally. Enjoyed doing the delivery in five different styles from varying points in front. Our woman sang her first line, joined in by one of the men for line two.

Went fast, me last. We all bowed together. Standing applause from the room.

We won the vote unanimously.

The next day, the President came by laughing. The Head of the trainers group said that they had complaints from a few of the companies their administrators came from. Said that he had sent a *"ringer"* in his place to win that final vote.

No fair sending a psychologist.

Exit

Late August. The end of my fourth year. I was at the annual psychology convention. In my absence, the president, fresh back from his own summer vacation, was in direct charge of my area, of everything. Not hard to do since the students were mostly gone and the faculty were on vacation. Just staff and him.

The former Registrar told me later of his vacation ploy. Each summer he took his wife and adult daughter on vacation to another country. Charged everything to his personal American Express card. An amount equal to a full time staff person's annual salary. Along the way, he would recruit a new student from that country. Then, on returning, he would approve reimbursement for his American Express card as a recruitment category, thereby paying for his entire family vacation. To approve this with no awareness by anybody else, this had to be charged to his own executive budget. Which put his budget way over, something the Board might notice. So every summer's end, he would fire a staffer, then transferring their salary to rebalance his department's budget. We never knew why he fired somebody from his supervision area at exactly that time of year, every year.

Not this time. While I was gone, he gathered two of my best staffers, both women with essential jobs, the Registrar and the Academic Coordinator, and told them that one of them had to be let go for budget reasons. Let them decide which one of them would quit. None of them had done less than excellent work. They refused.

On my return the president, minus much explanation, just told me that there was a budget problem and one of these necessary positions must go, the inhabitant fired. He ordered me to do so. I declined. Said that would not be ethical. Frustrated, he fired me. Solved his budget dilemma.

I shrugged and called a mover for my office belongings. To keep your integrity, it's always wise to keep your bags packed as well.

On the way out, I said goodbye to Michael Butz, a graduate student overseeing the clinic. Who would expect people to be around in late August? Butz moved fast. As did Carl Word and other key faculty. Within a few days most students were there leading a public protest. Made the country's evening news.

Faculty leaders demanded and got a public meeting with the president. Faculty psychologist Etzel Cardena confronted him with direct questions. In response, as advised by his lawyer, he confirmed that I had done nothing illegal, unethical, or contrary to the survival of the school. He said we just parted over a difference of opinion.

After that, about half the faculty left in agreement with the departed students.

Not an easy time for all those who had left in protest. So many of these students were in their final year of their program. The protesting faculty had to find new jobs, an abrupt change in their chosen career.

Academic immigrants.

But they had left as a matter of conscience, of principle. Many key CEOs of Bay Area universities and organizations turned out to be persuadable, to welcome them in as proven to be exactly the highest integrity people they were looking for. I took a year to assist those who left the school in protest, students and faculty, find a better place to be.

Students completed their doctorates on time, in a new better setting. One, Ann Yabusaki, became the President of the new school she had completed her degree in. Michael Butz and so many of the rest changed the face of psychology for the better, guiding the human family into a 21st century world full of fresh challenges.

In that last year, departing faculty often formulated their own strategy, their own best solution. Talented creative people. Also needed leaders into the 21st century. I was there to help as needed. One of my best spent years.

In the end we all eventually did better.

No more drama.

We learned that when we fall, land higher.

Higher ground.

1990s
Credible

Theme: *I Still Believe* Tim Cappello (*The Lost Boys* movie)

Trust is the essence of any relationship that succeeds. It comes in at least three basic kinds of credibility

Credible- You believe.

Non-Credible- You do not.

Incredible- Always a big surprise.

Sympathetic Enchantment

Themes: *Magic Music* Peter Gundry; *Magic* Olivia Newton-John

"James George Frazer coined the term "sympathetic magic" in The Golden Bough (1889); Richard Andree, however, anticipated Frazer, writing of sympathy-enchantment (German: Sympathie-Zauber) in his 1878 Ethnographische Parallelen und Vergleiche. Frazer subcategorized sympathetic magic into two varieties: that relying on similarity, and that relying on contact or "contagion": If we analyze the principles of thought on which magic is based, they will probably be found to resolve themselves into two: first, that like produces like, or that an effect resembles its cause; and, second, that things which have once been in contact with each other continue to act on each other at a distance after the physical contact has been severed. The former principle may be called the Law of Similarity, the latter the Law of Contact or Contagion. From the first of these principles, namely the Law of Similarity, the magician infers that he can produce any effect he desires merely by imitating it."

-Wikipedia

1990, Billings Montana. My first year at what is now part of the Montana State University system. I called us new faculty 'the freshman class' and it caught on.

In my new apartment, I taped a favorite page from a very old daily calendar to inside my refrigerator. It explained that opening the refrigerator door for five minutes was better for the machine's cooling than opening and closing the door five times in five minutes. The daily date on that past outdated page was April 17th, announced in large print.

I met a new librarian in my freshman class cohort. We hit it off. A little later she visited my apartment for the first time. Walked into the kitchen. Opened refrigerator door. Said: *"Why do you have MY BIRTHDAY inside your refrigerator?"* Now, at this writing, we have been together for 35 years.

The Porcelain Protector

Theme: *Constipation Blues* Screamin' Jay Hawkins

"I call this 'fighting without fighting'." Bruce Lee in *Enter the Dragon*.

In psychotherapy as well as in the rest of life, change does begin with yourself. If it ends there, it is often incomplete. Trauma does not always disappear with understanding. Action resolving these feelings can be very helpful. A safe kind of fighting back. Such real life interventions, when facilitated by a therapist, were called "Radical Therapy" in the 1970s.

Or "Nonviolent Direct Action" in Civil Rights progress. Martin Luther King knew this well. He was all about action, nonviolent action, in a just cause to right a wrong. In his day, laws were passed to suppress voting, remove freedoms, oppress women and racial minorities, ban books. Wait. In HIS day? Well. Anyway, Dr. King advocated an alternate choice to obeying an unjust law. Break it openly, in plain sight, preferably with 'newspaper reporters' (ask your grandfather) watching. Be willing to go to jail or at least be arrested in order to call attention from a public conscience (grandmother will elaborate) and, awareness raised, ultimately fix the problem. Also, even just trying meant that this direct action was good for you. Good for your wellbeing and mental health. Dr. King often told us it was good for the soul.

Today I see this as an important real world option to end PTSD in a satisfying manner- let's call this phase "Resolution". The therapist is more than a catalyst here. Finding resolution requires that the action be just, legal, ethical, and consistent with the action taker's morals, Oh, and if possible, fun too. Aside from psychotherapy, this push back option fits real civilian life even better.

It was in the beginning years of the last decade in the 20th century. We were engaged to get married, both of us working at a Montana university. Before we departed, a few of our friends gathered to wish us luck. One, Ron, a told us this story from his former life in the Secret Service:

"This American military officer was in charge of his captured men in a World War Two German concentration camp. His rank granted him decent health care plus access to the German commandant. His diabetes had grown worse there and his left leg was amputated. The officer asked the commandant to send the lost leg to his family back in America for proper burial. That was approved and done. As was the remaining leg when it too had to be amputated. In time, the disease

was reported as growing worse. Now the left arm was scheduled for amputation. Again the commandant was asked to send the lost arm to the officer's family back in the United States. This time the German commandant stormed into the officer's quarters with the written request in his hand. He yelled: 'I KNOW WHAT YOU ARE DOING! YOU ARE TRYING TO ESCAPE!' "

We took this to mean support for our exit. Maybe.

Our first stop, on the way to California, was at an Idaho university.

My fiancé began a reference librarian job there while I waited for my Idaho psychology license to be approved. It was most challenging for her.

Her immediate supervisor was a single parent with marital hopes. He routinely called her in on Saturdays or Sundays though not her regular shift. His supervisor was attracted to my fiancé as a lesbian opportunity, planning an auto tour for the two of them at the first opportunity. The worst was the overall supervisor, the library's Dean. I was told by staff right away that he saw women working under him to fulfill that very position as sexually as it pleased him.

While my fiancé fended off the triple threats as diplomatically as possible, all three supervisors saw me as the obstacle. Especially the Dean.

Knowing that my credential to practice psychology might take weeks to arrive, I spent much time in the library. Lunches with my fiancé, reading, interacting with staff.

The Dean put out a written order on his stationary to staff that I was not allowed to read or be near the psychology section of the library. No explanation but the message was clear. Open to public or not, I was unwelcome.

I complied but was not discouraged.

I kept visiting every day in other sections.

The Dean countered that by alerting staff and campus law enforcement that I was a theft risk. Again by written decree on his stationary.

I was therefore watched carefully, especially at the exits, cameras included, to make sure I was leaving with no equipment.

A friendly staffer, the Dean's secretary said, if I really was a thief, to take the Dean's newest and very expensive printer, housed in the hall just outside his office. She was angry at the Dean for his unwelcome advances. Had put a Christmas photo of him with his wife and children on her desk, ready for pointing as needed.

I thanked her for the advice but I really wasn't a thief.

Still.

One afternoon, outside camera range, I picked up the printer outside his office and put it inside the empty bottom drawer of his jumbo file cabinet next to it.

Then walked empty handed out the front of the library in view of the security cameras.

The apparent disappearance of the Dean's deluxe printer became a cause.

On entry to the library thereafter, a librarian was assigned to follow me at all times.

When I entered at the front, I took the stairs to the second floor. He followed.

Then I was on to the elevator to the basement.

After he got there, I went back on the elevator to the top floor.

I waited for him there.

He said he was supposed to report to the Dean everything I did, particularly if I tried to go near the off-limits psychology section, and, yes, if I stole anything.

He asked me to slow down as he was winded chasing me.

I suggested he take off for an hour and rest. Said I would stay on the main floor in plain sight for exactly one hour. He thanked me, agreed.

On the main floor, I stopped to talk to the Dean's secretary. The one ready to point to the photo of the Dean's wife and children to her boss as needed.

She had packed up her things in a box. Leaving at the end of the day to get married in another state.

Still two hours to go. But she could leave early once she finished this last onerous task.

She showed me a blank page of the Dean's stationary with his signature at the bottom. Her regular job was to write a library piece for him each week and then drop it in the mail box to be published in the university campus newsletter.

She had been told to do this, even on her last day.

But she had ghost writer's block.

I volunteered to do a draft for her. This I did.

She loved it, filled the blank part of the page just over the Dean's signature with it.

Sealed it in a library envelope addressed to the newsletter.

Dropped it in the campus mail.

She left work early that day, never to return.

My hour ended soon after. Time to give my Dean-anointed shadow another workout.

The letter was dutifully published.

The campus populace read it. Went something like this:

Capable versus Culpable

Our hardworking library maintenance crew devotes each night to cleaning our rest rooms. In this they are first rate, making the porcelain sinks and toilets spotless, shining, pure. A work of art. Such capable porcelain artists. But in the morning, all their work is reversed. Users of the facilities soil the porcelain beyond belief, all day long. Toilets and sinks must be scrubbed all over again. And it is not a pleasant challenge for our so capable late night cleaners. Consequently it is my responsibility as Dean of the Library to rein in our culpable visitors. Yes, admire our books, engage our staff, appreciate our building. But, from now on, DO NOT USE OUR RESTROOMS.

No more soiling the porcelain. All rest rooms will be locked during the day with the exception of authorized tours to admire the sanitation artistry of our evening staff. Your cooperation is mandated. *Signed by the Dean of the library plus name and title*

Well. It made him campus famous. It made his secretary happy for once, at last.

For me, the memory still glows.

Some years later.

My wife and I both worked in the Bay Area of California during the week and then spent the weekends in our new house a drive of many hours away, in Chico at the edge of mountain country.

So we rented a small first floor apartment in a complex just walking distance from my job. It was in a quiet section, apart from the other apartments.

We faced three young beautiful trees and had wonderful next door neighbors. They had come from a small Asian country. Maintained the Pacific Rim cultural custom of leaving their shoes just outside their front door so as to not track in anything that might damage the internal carpet.

Thanks to the trees in front of us, nobody could see the shoes but us.

We appreciated their custom, appreciated their friendliness, admired their drive to succeed in this new country.

But the manager was not happy. Left a note on their front door to no longer leave shoes in front of that door. Said they would be evicted for creating this eyesore if they did not immediately comply.

I went to her front office and asked her to relent. Said the only people that could see the shoes were us and we thought it was fine. The three trees in front of our apartments masked the view from any other tenants. She said she would consider this.

The next day she had the young trees cut down.

Our neighbors moved their shoes to a mat just inside their front door and were not evicted.

The manager then put out a regular note on her stationary, distributed to shelves above the mailboxes of all tenants. She let us all know of her victory against shoe clutter.

I visited her again, angry as I almost never am.

She surprised me. She took my hands in hers and turned on the charm. She was probably in her 30s and, despite her obnoxious decisions, physically attractive. Married, she still was clearly seeking more. And said so.

I freed my hands and reminded her: *"We're both married, right?"*

Her response: *"But NOT to each other! That's the best part!"*

When I declined, she shifted gears. Said she was honored to have me as a tenant, loved my books. She said she would still show me *real* appreciation if I helped her with a project.

She wanted me to write the next tenant community note for her. The theme was to economize. The owners were pressuring her to cut expenses and increase revenue- more for less. Saw me as a solution to her problem. So she gave me a blank community note form with her office logo and her name at the top.

Leaning close, she reminded me that she would be *very* grateful in a personal way I would not forget. Once my note persuaded the tenants to cut costs.

I took the form. Left.

It reminded me of that Idaho porcelain protector event.

I filled out her form, and distributed her stationary statement to the shelves above all the tenant mailboxes as follows:

> **As you know, from time to time, we must economize. To save on our water bill, we are banning the taking of any showers in all apartments. All shower heads will be sealed. In respect for your own hygiene, we are going to schedule time as needed in the swimming pool on a first come first served basis. You can sign up for a ten minute cleansing swim at the front office.**

Well. We were moving out by then anyway,

The Comet Hunter

Themes: *Corcovado (Quiet Nights of Quiet Stars)* Astrud Gilberto; *What It's Like Being Married to Neil deGrasse Tyson* Key & Peele

July 1994. Astronomers Carolyn and Gene Shoemaker with their colleague, celebrated science writer David Levy, saw the comet they had discovered the year before crash into Jupiter, our largest planet.

Photo by Chris Butler/Science Photo Library

That extra year gave scientists and media time to prepare for this unique celestial event. But nobody was prepared for the traffic accident that killed Gene Shoemaker and severely hospitalized his wife three years later. David Levy continued their work in Flagstaff, Arizona, including television appearances, first about the comet, next about the Shoemaker couple. He went on to discover 22 more comets to earn the title of *Comet Hunter*. His 34 books include *David Levy's Guide to the Night Sky*, *The Quest for Comets*, a biography of Pluto-discoverer Clyde Tombaugh in 2006, and his tribute to Gene Shoemaker in *Shoemaker by Levy,* plus magazine articles for *Sky and Telescope*, *Parade*, *Sky News,* and *Astronomy*. Among many other honors, he received the Smithsonian Astrophysical Observatory's Edgar Wilson Award for the discovery of comets. In 2008, he co-designed a special edition telescope, "**The Comet Hunter**". He has promoted the study of night-time astronomy for the public in a variety of programs and opportunities. David is likely the most significant proponent for understanding what we are seeing in the night skies.

This was a special moment. When David Levy came on our television news, I turned to my wife Becky and said with delight: *"Hey! That's David. He was my student in my Canadian university days. Nova Scotia in the late 1960s. From Montreal. He made a great career of his choices then."* She thought I was kidding. I shrugged. Said we would see. I did nothing and left it to fate. We moved on. Three months later, David knocked on our front door.

He had come a long way to say thank you. He said I was one of the three professors that had mattered most to his future. In my case, we had worked on blending what he really enjoyed doing, literature and astronomy, into what a future career might look like. He had followed that path. And, because that's what David Levy is like, he took the time to say thanks. We've been in touch ever since.

Becky took this in stride and was a gracious host. We didn't discuss it much after David's visit. I may have had a smirk. Tried not to.

But these events in life are more than Karmic. They are contagious. As the years rolled on in our marriage, my proportion of being right plateaued. No better, no worse. Becky's proportion of being right improved with each passing year. Until not long ago, she surpassed me. Wisdom had struck in her sixties. These days I pay great attention to her ideas, predictions, creations. No need to wait for a comet. Or another knock on our front door.

My celebrity lives here.

Valentine's Day
at the San Francisco Zoo

Themes: *Lioness Roar* Adventure Specialist; *The Lion Sleeps Tonight Wimoweh* Miriam Makeba/ Pete Seeger & the Weavers

Peacocks walking everywhere at the San Francisco Zoo. It was in the early 1990s that year we went to the end-of-day *Couples Valentine* event there.

As we went by each animal lair, we were regaled with their mating habits. We especially noted the male lion surrounded by his harem. The females did the hunting for him, at night. It seemed to us that the small moat and smaller fence around them would not keep these lionesses in once nocturnal dinner time happened.

At the end of the event, we gathered up our souvenirs and prizes to slip away from the exiting crowd. We wanted to see the Gorillas as they had been missed. Meanwhile the zoo closed. We were alone, walking past the lion exhibit. The lionesses were up and pacing while the sun began to set.

Once past them, we noticed the peacocks had stopped moving, gathered together here and there.

The sunset was ending and darkness beginning.

Behind us we heard a roar from the direction of the lionesses.

Suddenly all the peacocks rose in a vertical flight cloud of beauty.

Then safely nested in the trees, every one.

We decided at that moment to skip seeing the gorillas and made for the only working exit, a side door that only opened outward to disgorge latecomers like us.

What the peacock eyes saw after that we never knew.

Anger: Three Cases

Theme: *Hold on I'm Coming* Eric Clapton, B.B. King, David Porter, Isaac Hayes/Sam & Dave

Years ago, I was a flatlander new to the mountain country of Northern California. As a psychologist in a region with no other psychologists, my work had the range of a country doctor. Time after time I was confronted with new challenges in this practice, ones outside my experience and expertise. Knowing that most of my patients felt that leaving their home territory for a city referral was like falling off the edge of the earth, I acknowledged that whatever I could contribute was likely the best they could get. I learned a lot and was more helpful than I had anticipated. (In fairness, some outlaws did go far enough down-altitude to raid stores in the Chico area.)

Case #1

Themes: *Wild Thing* Troggs/Sam Kinison/Jimi Hendrix; *Something to Talk About* Bonnie Raitt

Let's call him *"Range"*. He was tall, wide, young, intense. Obviously suppressing some rage. Sat facing me and scowled.

Range said his wife had referred him to me for his uncontrollable violent anger. He was always attacking people for the slightest reason. Just the day before he had told her that he was going to beat up her hospital surgeon. That's when she insisted he come see me first. And here he was.

It wasn't hard to relax Range. First I acknowledged that he looked angry. He agreed and stopped looking that way, interested in the conversation now.

In a few minutes he was smiling. He had asked me before we began if I was married and if I loved my wife. After my two yes answers, he unclenched his fists and said that he was ready to begin the session.

I asked him why he wanted to attack his wife's surgeon.

Range explained that he loved his wife so overwhelmingly that he just wanted to protect her. She was a little over-weight and he felt he had to fight anybody who hurt her feelings about that. The surgeon had given her a diagnostic spinal tap, no problem found, which then caused her continuing pain. The surgeon just told her that she had to live with hurt and not whine about it all the time. Clearly he had decided that this doctor needed a bloody nose consequence.

As an expert in fighting iatrogenic malpractice, medical mistakes, I understood his feelings fully. It was important though to help him learn to fight back in a less destructive way to himself and his wife. A goal too often skipped by therapists.

We focused on the consequences, following visualizations of that intended fight. Visualizing an attack actually reduced the anger, added control. Nobody ever gets arrested for a private thought (so far). He liked the technique. We tried it on me as the target. By then the relationship between us had become friendly and even a mental vision of an attack on me was hard for him to do. He settled for imagining a pie in my face and we both laughed.

Now he came in for a few more once a week sessions, glad to share his control. But he still had lots of suppressed rage he carried with him. He asked me why. This was his real goal for therapy: to understand himself. I agreed as it also would give him even more control.

I'm not much of a follower of Freudian doctrine other than saluting him as an essential ancient pioneer for our profession. Most helpful though for me was the emphasis on a problem's origin. *"When did this first begin?"* and *"What was going on then?"* are often useful questions. The emotions felt then and now of course.

Range learned to relax in the chair, shut his eyes, and visualize the answer.

That took him back to a time in his early years when his mother remarried. The stepfather often beat him as a child. It stopped, as it often does, when Range had grown as big as his stepfather. But the child's rage was still ever with him. Also the violent model he had learned from his oppressive stepfather.

On reflection, no, he didn't want to be like him.

Well, not like the way his violent stepfather had been before..

What has changed now?

Oh, he said, they go fishing together at least once a week. They get along okay then.

Has he ever apologized? No.

Did you ever bring the beatings up when you were fishing? Remind him? No.

I suggested he might do that next time they were off fishing together.

Range grinned and said he liked the idea.

(If I had this to do again, with Range's approval, I would have arranged for the stepfather to come into a session with Range to accomplish this. Hindsight is not always helpful, coming as late as the word sounds, sometimes direct from the hind quarters of our anatomy. Meaning- I was wrong.)

Range entered our next session limping. He had a black eye, cuts, bruises, and a bandage on his forehead. But he was ecstatic.

Said he had reminded his stepfather of all that childhood abuse. Said the old boy had put up quite a fight but in the end Range won the struggle. The stepfather apologized on his way to the hospital. Recovered in a few days later. No more fishing dates though.

On our last session, Range brought his wife.

They both agreed that Range was civilized now.

Said they had never been happier.

I didn't ask about the stepfather's opinion.

Case #2

Themes: *The Sopranos* Alabama 3; *The Lion Sleeps Tonight Wimoweh* Miriam Makeba; *Walk on the Wild Side instrumental* Jimmy Smith

He was a high ranking law enforcer from another rural county. Let's call him "*Shane*".

Personable and wearing a cowboy hat (no cattle), he sat easily in the guest chair. Said he had come once before to my clinic but my associate had not impressed him.

That other person doing counseling had no academic credentials beyond a college degree or any psychotherapy training, but was a relentlessly nice person. He was the best they had to see clients wanting therapy before I got there. After my joining him, I left him more time for his hobby: constructing homes for his neighbors. That made him very happy.

Back to Shane.

Shane took off his hat, smiled, and said he had heard about me being helpful to many and, besides, able to keep confidences.

Still, a psychologist's clients have not the absolute confidentiality enjoyed by lawyers and clergy. I showed him the printed exceptions of state law, including (1) convincing dangerousness to self or others, and (2) convincing confession of serious crime.

(I once counseled an elderly woman who in retirement had pulled off some impressive department store shoplifting as a hobby. Never caught. Yet. And this made *her* happy. Seemed to be seeing me to brag in confidence. We did find an even happpier hobby that was without risk of her arrest.)

Shane considered these exceptions carefully, glancing at me several times and rereading the exceptions on the paper.

Finally he carefully phrased the following: *"I'm here to see you to help me with my sadness. Losing sleep over it. It's a very cold case. Many years ago a man was killed in a late night fight behind a bar.*

About then I joined the law but I never caught the killer. I still feel guilty about that. Maybe you can help me shed that guilt."

Shane handed me back the confidentiality exceptions paper. Raised an eyebrow to see if I understood.

I considered. Seemed like he was the killer he wanted to discuss. But there was no evidence for this to justify any legal intervention. Onward then.

I said I would help him.

I had Shane sit back, shut his eyes, and go into a light trance for visualization.

Asked him to imagine he was in the mind of the killer.

This he did, signaling he was there.

So I asked him the key question: *"Will he ever kill again, then or now?"*

A vehement no. My relief.

"So exactly what happened the night of the crime. Let him tell us."

Shane described a late night when, leaving the bar at the back, a larger man demanded his money. Rage overcame him, plus maybe he had drunk too much. The rest was unclear. He just remembered standing over the body and then disappearing into the night. He was confused, frightened.

Shane woke up at that point, sitting tall in his chair.

He said that was all he could get from this memory. Except that when the body was found the next day, this was to be his first case. But no witnesses, never solved. Haunted him still.

Shane came back for his weekly sessions. By the second month he had grown quite adept at describing the thought and feelings of his quarry, a man much like himself. Maybe exactly like himself.

He went on to speak in his imagination with the victim.

Who in the end forgave the killer.

Shane shared his own just and successful law career over the years. Raised a family and became a valued neighbor.

He explored the consequences if his killer just confessed the crime. Imagined several different paths. In the end, he shared that his nightmares had gone away and a blanket of peace slipped over him each night. He said that maybe the killer would confess to law some day but that decision could wait. The killer coming out with everything in our sessions had given Shane relief. Time to live in the present.

Our last session.

As to the killer in his mind, he was gone now. His rage had never come back, and he never drank again after that incident. No, Shane said, nor had he himself.

He thought the killer might some day want to connect again in his imagination. Maybe at night when he slept.

I asked him how he would react.

He said he had already imagined this.

The killer would say *"Shane! Come back Shane!"*

But he would just ride off into the horizon, into the decent life where he belonged.

Case #3

Themes: *Yojimbo opening theme; Crying* Roy Orbison & KD Lang

This last case takes us to Hawaii in the mid-1960s where I was doing my post-doc internship at the Hawaii State Hospital.

My supervisor acknowledged my success so far with adult patients and with my adolescent day program, a therapeutic community for 30 teens that had never had an unfortunate incident in its yearlong history. So he said I needed some humility, a failure experience. He assigned me to what he termed a psychotic paranoid patient who would never recover.

He was big, Japanese-American and considered dangerous. Scowling as he entered my office, he looked like Toshiro Mifune, the iconic screen samurai.

Though we were both only in our 20s.

So we'll call him "Tosh".

Tosh had returned to his family after being thrown out of the Marines. Shameful for them already. But then he began to listen for hours to Japanese radio stations. Strange because he knew no Japanese language. He insisted they were talking about him and were truly insulting. Rage built up by the day until he went down to the station and attacked the staff.

At first the police, following a judge's order, just brought him home to await his trial. That didn't last long. A few more rage issues and he was committed to the state mental hospital. Involuntarily

in a strait jacket. It took six orderlies. In front of neighbors. Overwhelming shame.

Loss of face came to any Japanese-American family there and then that included a "crazy" member. So most did all they could to keep their own out of sight and away from the state mental hospital. This meant that fewer ethnic Japanese patents inhabited the state hospital but those that were there were so out-of-control that the families had given up.

Tosh had heard from other patients that my office was a safe place so he was cautious but curious, suppressing hs obvious anger. The hidden fear below this anger remaining to be discovered.

After some small talk, he chose to explain his view. Everybody in the world was out to get him. Or, the few exceptions, maybe me, were just foolishly unaware of that reality.

Tosh then took it upon himself to instruct me about this conspiracy that was all around us. I listened carefully and with respect. At the core of every paranoid fantasy was a personal reality. One we needed to find.

Clearly, his view of himself as bravely standing aginst an entire world on his own, well, it functioned as a shield against his sad temporary reality.

We shared some light food which also helped Tosh relax. I answered his questions about me and my life to date. This included my honest response that I didn't agree with his conviction that all the world was against him. Instead I told him that likely he had definitely been wronged at points in his past.

This candor built trust as we now agreed to disagree about the nature of his delusion.

He said he looked forward to more meetings. And better food next time.

Our second session, with appetizers more to his taste, went better. He now wanted very much to explain to me how he been wronged, what had brought him to this day in the hospital.

First though, he wanted some help in controlling his rage. One doctor had wanted him lobotomized, another favored eletroconvulsive therapy. Clearly he wanted to avoid these damaging things. If he hurt one more orderly he would be punished with destructive interventions. He has read about all these "treatments".

I was impressed. There was in fact a very good mind hiding in the paranoia.

We went through breathing exercises and visualization techniques for more control of his anger. Fight rather than flight had been his remedy. Or maybe both combined.

Tosh excelled at these methods, even allowing himself a smile when done. He knew he was a quick study which I confirmed. Again I was impressed. For him, his success in my office was a minor windfall in the midst of great disaster.

By the remainder of that session and into the next he shared his life to that point. He labeled this narrative variously as being in "*Deep Kimchi*" or "*Up the Yinyang*".

Tosh shared an early memory. He was a toddler sitting under a tree when a falling coconut smashed into his young head. A serious potentially lethal hazard. Likely a concussion. But when he regained consciousness, his older sisters were there laughing at him. His scalp was full of blood, which they thought was hilarious. Still hurt his head to remember.

Now we were getting to the core of his paranoid universe: the actual world that *was* against him: his family when he was a child.

Worse was life growing up with his father. Since his father spoke no English and Tosh didn't understand Japanese, there was literally no communication. Father did do much harsh discipline to his son though Tosh never knew why. His mother would not help him. Nor his sisters.

Now his actual world was coming into focus. His childhood must have seemed the whole universe to him. An unjust world demanding he project some meaning into it.

He did well though in school. Became strong and athletic. Loved reading. On graduating high school, he joined the Marines, something that he thought might impress his family.

Marine basic training is meant to collapse a recruit's personality and rebuild it as a warrior. This occurs by pushing their physical and mental limits to beyond what they can stand. Tosh, vulnerable to begin with, had an extra problem.

His trainers thought he was an American Indian. Called him *"blanket-back"*. Tosh didn't let them know any different for a very good reason. His trainers had served in WW2, in the war against Japan. Just two decades before. They remembered Pearl Harbor. Japanese-American trainees would get a whole extra layer of destruction if they were discovered.

Tosh was discovered.

He was once more in an unjust world. He fought back. Hard.

Dishonorable discharge.

Home to his family in Hawaii.

There he began listening to those Japanese language radio stations, delusionally thinking he understood what they were saying.

I asked Tosh in our session what he thought they were saying. In this way we could understand the fear underlying his violent anger.

They were announcing to the world that he was a *"Mahu"* which means effeminate or a homosexual. This in 1960s Hawaii, especially to his family and the Japanese-American community, was a blood insult. It was seen as a perversion, either predatory or to be laughed at.

Tosh had used his rage to prove them wrong with violence. That's when he went to one of the radio stations to attack the station manager and dj. The same next at the other Japanese language station before the police caught up to him. Charges included several of the hospitalized officers who had trouble arresting him.

A psychiatrist had him certified insane so he was transferred to the state mental hospital for an indeterminate time. Possibly for life.

Tosh had finished his story. He was calm while in my office and had a request.

Could he help me with my work?

I was collecting library material on shock treatment's damaging side effects which eventually became a book *"Electroshock: The Case*

Against". But at that early stage, the task was to gather the science. I did a study ccomparing patients who had been given ECT with similar ones who had not. ECT survivors had damaged memories of two kinds. They forgot key parts of their life sometimes including people they loved. They also forget new information, meaning it was hard to learn. Nor did ECT do any lasting good for their diagnostic condition, even in one case with a violent patient where he received 300 shocks (and was still violent). There was a near perfect correlation though between when a patient hit a staff memnber and that patient next receiving ECT. A punishment? Clearly so.

Tosh had been threatened with ECT and really wanted to avoid it. So he gladly became my research assistant and haunted the hospital library for material.

Now he had a purpose and improved substantially. He had accepted that the reality core for his paranoia was in his own personal world and not in the earth's entire human population. He got very good at understanding his anger and channeling it in an effective but legal manner.

Plus he really was helpful to my work.

So much so that I was able to persuade the staff of my unit to close down any ECT. Our psychiatrist-in-charge had not been there for an extended period of months. On his return he went along, reluctantly, with the ECT ban though it truly was the only psychiatry he knew how to do. Let's just say that he was far from happy with me.

Tosh eventually had improved so much that I got him a discharge to leave the hospital, a *"conditional discharge"* which allowed him to return once a week so he could continue our weekly meetings, ones he worked on assimilating to his community. He enrolled in a university counseling degree program while living in the dormitory there. He managed some decent interactions with his sisters, now also in their own adult lives.

Tosh was doing fine.

My supervisor conceded that I had failed to receive sufficient humility. I assured him that I had already more than enough failures in life for humility and expected some valuable learning from much more in the future. I still think he had been rooting for Tosh to get better all along, hence his humility challenge.

One of my own supervisees, intern Jerry Shapiro, made sure I had a humility experience before I left. In my turn to demonstrate psychotherapy with a volunteer patient in front of staff and interns, Jerry chose for me a lobotomized patient. (Volunteer?) Nothing useful came of this demo. Well, maybe some humility.

One week Tosh came in for his weekly meeting looking really stressed.

He said: *"Doc you won't believe this. But on the bus on the way here today some girls were laughing at me. I did NOT imagine this!"*

What did he do about it?

"I just waited to tell you about it. I ignored the girls completely."

Feelings at the time?

"I couldn't wait to tell you. I was afraid that I was getting sick again. And I was, well, proud that I didn't get angry. Right?"

"Exactly. You should be proud. Now you can choose what to do with hurt or fear. Still, knowing why they laughed can help. Let's shine a light on it. Because, you know, I get why they laughed. Look at your tee shirt and shorts."

He did. His shirt and shorts were borrowed from a roommate in the dorm. Both too small tee and shorts had Mickey Mouse on them, somewhat incongruous on a powerful samurai-looking man.

Tosh looked, considered, and broke out in a loud laugh. He got it. And that laugh meant to me that he was really back to normal.

In another week's meeting, I asked him if there was anything in his recovery that stood out for him. He did have something he wanted to highlight.

"Doc, early on I asked you what I could possbily do when the whole world just gives me a pile of shit! You said 'plant flowers'. I think you might have been joking but I used that many times as a ladder to climb out into the sunshine, the fresh air smelling of flowers in our Hawaii."

We had our last outpatient meeting as I was on my way to a new job outside Hawaii. I gave Tosh my contact information so he could stay in touch, do followups, and let me know if he needed any other consultation. He returned to his studies.

With me gone, that psychiatrist-in-charge of the unit brought back into the ward his only tool: ECT. He systematically gave shock treatments to as many of my remaining former patients as he could. He had held up Tosh's full discharge long enough to call him back in. There he forced Tosh to undergo a series of three shock treatments.

He knew that Tosh would particularly suffer as now he had become an expert on the destructive risks of ECT. Tosh knew it was punitive. As did the shock doctor. Had I still been there, my own anger might well have gone violent. My visualizations worked overtime. I redoubled my anti-ECT work.

Tosh could have reverted to paranoia as this unfair world of punishing involuntary ECT was familiar. But instead he contacted me by phone.

I got his discharge to be final through my hospital network but the damage was done. Tosh had nearly completed his course work but there were still tests to pass. Now his memory for newly learned material was impaired. So he drew on library resources again. Used memory devices to get him through. Each morning he reviewed his written notes from the day before to restore the memories. He passed his exams.

Tosh moved to another state and took a job as a counselor there.

Every Christmas for ten years Tosh would send me a present with a note of thanks. I knew not to respond with more than a return thank you card. In the culture he grew up in, he was paying what he saw as a necessary debt.

On the tenth year I called him long distance at his office. We caught up on life. He finally asked if his gifts were enough. I confirmed that was so. Debt paid.

Tosh continued his work despite the memory challenges and must have helped thousands before he retired back to Hawaii before the 20th century's close.

He departed life five years into our 21st century and a full life it was after all.

The Raft

Theme: *Malagueña* Lucas Imbiriba (acoustic guitar)

The Bellagio Hotel, Las Vegas, Nevada, 1998. My wife sat with me in the front row, waiting for the Cirque du Soleil show to begin. It was a new show titled *"O"*, which when said out loud sounded like *"Eau"*, the French word for water. Made sense since the stage in front of us was primarily a small lake of water. A water circus.

She had dressed up. Her, always both elegant and beautiful. Me, in my late forties, wearing the three piece suit, masquerading as "dignified". That and a substantial tip to the man seating us got our front row view. Close enough to get wet if need be.

On with the show. Lights low. Spotlights. The water ballets and numbers were magnificent, colorful, energetic, amazing.

Then the stage lake cleared and a small raft came into view. It was propelled by two standing hobos in tattered clothes and porkpie hats. One tall and one short. They pushed their raft forward, all the way to the edge closest to us. Crowd quiet, interested, waiting.

The taller hobo then stepped off to the edge of the dry stage. Held his hand out to me. Motioned to me to join him on the raft. Spotlight surrounded us.

Why me? The suit? But yes, I would go.

Becky squeezed my hand, meaning she would support me if I went on stage or support me if I choose to fight our way out of the auditorium. Held her hand for a second.

Thanks much, love.

And got up to join the hobos on their raft.

In that second I had a memory flash. My lifelong friend, psychologist and hypnotist Leonard Elkind, told me of a time when he had been pulled onto a dance floor with a beautiful skilled Flamenco dancer. One he didn't know at all. As the spotlight hit just them, Len took on a new Spanish personality. Imagined himself a practiced Flamenco dancer. Which somehow worked. Applause when they finished.

I had seen this technique of a substitute persona for learning a new language. But not for an unrehearsed stage performance. Still, in that moment of getting up from my seat and stepping on stage, I knew I was an actor, part of that act. As some deity intended.

I stepped on the raft, surrounded by water. Comfortable in my persona as a stiff middle aged man in a three piece suit. Slow acoustic guitar music. I was dancing, in a dignified confident way with the shorter hobo.

Round and round, in tune with the music.

When the music stopped, we did too. I bowed to both of my new raft friends. They returned it.

I stepped off the raft and back to my seat in the front row. Spotlight still on me, I turned to the audience, bowed to them, and then sat.

Loud applause.

The hobos pushed off and out of the spotlight to disappear from the stage lake.

Lights dimmed for the next act.

Becky turned to me and leaned toward my nearest ear.

Saying *"That was brave! But who ARE you?"*

I just said *"Me? Oh. He's gone now."*

Crossover

Themes: *Fire* Pointer Sisters; *Light My Fire* Jose Feliciano/Doors
Greenville burned to the ground not long ago.

Before, it had been a small town in the majestic Maidu Indian Country of northern California's mountains, just miles below the Lake Almanor reservoir. Here as it was:

The closest city was a two hour drive to Reno. Other American Indian tribes were present here and there, plus some white self-styled "*Outlaw*" bands that descended occasionally to pillage the "*flat-landers*" in Chico.

Back in the late 1990s a small clinic was established for the under-served people of Greenville. I was the only psychologist in that half of the county, so it kept me busy.

J was one of my patients. A white woman in her 40s, originally born in Wisconsin, she had lived her adult life in Greenville with her husband, a pet household pig, and friendly neighbors. Everybody liked J. I was no exception. She was the first to share this expression with me regarding her spouse "that *he always gets his panties in a bunch*". She carefully described her home wood stove as consisting of just three basic parts: *"Lifter, Leg, and Poker"*, followed by an endearing laugh.

Her problems were resolvable much as her visits were enjoyable. My wife gladly drove her past the Greenville known limits of the universe (Chico again) to a medical referral in Oakland.

One weekly visit stood out. She had been in the waiting room where she overheard some teenage clients happily discussing their new *"Spirit Guides"*. These were specific animals that they consulted in dreams or trance for key decisions. One boy had his own talking fox while the other had a helpful raccoon.

Teaching them how to do this was a technique I learned from Eduardo Duran's work in Indian Country near Fresno. Supervising him taught me a lot.

Now, some might just say this was only a way to harness imagination in order to generate best choices. Others experienced it literally. Either way, it was valuable, useful, and a definite client mood elevator.

J wanted me to teach her how to have her own Spirit Guide. I explained that it belonged within a tribal culture with respect. Her own perspective likely wouldn't fit or work. Hard to say no to J though so: by the end of our hour she had learned the method, left happy.

The following week she entered my office looking confused.

She said: *"It worked okay but my Spirit Guide is human and still alive."*

And: *"It was Eddie Murphy."*

Working with JFK

Theme: *The Good, the Bad, and the Ugly* Danish National Symphony Orchestra.

I was offered a thousand dollars to never enter the JFK library again.

The University

John F. Kennedy or JFK was our 35th[th] president. Much loved and respected by millions, deservedly so. When he was running for that office in 1960, I voted for president the first time.

Not for JFK or for Nixon but for Dick Gregory of the Peace and Freedom Party. My first and last third party vote.

But I never met that JFK. I was only 22 when he was assassinated in 1963. By then I had realized his great value to our human family.

No, but in the 1994-1995 school year more than 30 years later, my wife Becky and I did work at a place called JFK University.

It was housed in the San Francisco Bay Area, thousands of miles west of where President JFK had worked and lived.

Nor did it have any direct connection to JFK or his family.

"John F. Kennedy University, located in Pleasant Hill, California, was named in honor of President John F. Kennedy. It was established in 1964, shortly after Kennedy's assassination, as a tribute to his vision of a more just and equitable society. While the university was not directly affiliated with Kennedy himself or his family, its name and mission reflect his ideals and principles, particularly in the realm of social justice and public service."

– GPT-4, 2024

The Job

Living not far from the JFK University, and knowing a treasured friend, Dr. Ann Yabusaki, was faculty there, we applied.

Becky was hired full time as a reference librarian for the JFK Library.

I was hired to teach an undergraduate night class on Lifespan Psychology.

The Library

Becky was always great at this job, professional but attentive, helpful, encouraging. So she was surprised when the Head Librarian told her to not be so *"patron friendly"*, meaning help for faculty and students coming to the library for assistance. *"Let them wait longer, teach them patience"* she ordered Becky.

The Head Librarian exemplified this request. She regularly ignored those waiting at the counter. Often brought her leashed dogs to work and concentrated on them much of the time. Had parties with friends in plain sight of patrons not being attended to. Came to light soon that Becky had been hired so quickly because of the high turnover of past reference librarians under the Head Librarian.

Becky stuck it out as best she could. But still stayed helpful to patrons.

The Night Class

The students were bright and motivated, mostly nurses, military, mothers, day workers. They took to the seminar fully and the once-a-week three hour session moved quickly through the material. Except for that first night.

One woman in the class was taking copious notes and never looked up. Without my permission, she was obviously recording the session. Nor was her name on my class register.

During a break I asked her why her name was missing. She said she was just there on assignment from the JFK president to make sure that nothing improper was being taught.

I asked what her verdict was. She shrugged and said it was *"up to him"*.

She left before the end of the class and never came back to it. A student told me that she was the president's secretary. Her boss was an attorney, so he kept a tight watch.

Never particularly meaning to avoid being improper, I apparently had passed this surveillance. For then.

The Nurse

During a break in my night class, I visited the library. My required books were on reserve where they should be. My wife was on days so only the Head Librarian was, in theory, on duty. But in fact the library, though open for night students, was uninhabited.

Except for one student, not in my course, a woman looking in her 60s, who was weeping quietly at the only table with this large sign: *"NIGHT STUDENTS SIT HERE- ALL OTHER TABLES ARE ONLY FOR FACULTY OR STAFF"*.

She apologized for crying but said she must be too old to be a student, had to accept this. Why? She said that even with her glasses she just wasn't able to read her textbook. She was a nurse on day shifts and needed this class.

The library was dimly lit at night and the bulb above her table had burned out. I had just covered this phase of life in my lifespan class and was glad to put it to use.

I said *"As we get older we just need more light to see things or read. Your eyes are okay. It's the lightbulb that got too old. Let's move to a place with more light. No, its fine. How about that brightly lit Staff table?"*

We moved to a staff-signed table where the light was better. Now she could read just fine. Smiles. Thanks.

The Thousand Dollar Light Bulb

The next day, late afternoon I stopped by the library to see the Head Librarian. She was never there in the mornings. I had told Becky about the nurse and the dead light bulb over the only student table but she said she'd been told that only the Head Librarian could authorize a request for any change.

I saw this special authorizer and showed her where the bulb's demise was handicapping night students at their only legitimate table. I politely suggested she might consider, besides getting a new light bulb, opening up other tables for night students. This didn't go over well.

She indignantly stressed that the signs and table assignment were hers to decide. Further, while she agreed the light bulb needed replacing, she would get to it when she was ready and not before. Added it was not my place as a temporary adjunct instructor, to have an opinion about this.

As I turned to leave, I wished her a good day and a *"Bless Your Heart"*, which I had learned was a powerful Southern curse. She seemed confused by this.

A week went by and it was time for another night with my class. I checked the library and saw that the deceased light bulb was still in place. As were the signs.

Realizing that I was, for then, actually staff, I turned in a written request to Maintenance to replace the light bulb. Becky told me that the next day it had been replaced. She was anticipating from her angry boss's silence that we would be as well, sooner rather than later.

HR Issues

Becky drew library hours nobody else wanted, including Saturday mornings. This left her off on Fridays from noon on.

By then I had a day job as a psychologist at an Oakland Clinic for Native Americans. Our staff there were invited to a Friday noon gathering which included interested patients and family. It would be hosted by the Native American Church. Becky and I naturally went.

It began with sweat lodge experiences, then the group gathering in a huge Teepee tent, open at the top, with optional hallucinogenic mushrooms (legalized by President Clinton for Native American church use) and sawdust for any consequent upset stomachs. Food was shared, prayers said, and the night found us all still there. We had become a close group, into a form of group process, sharing genuine feelings, fears, hope. By then it was clear that this staff gathering would last 24 hours, until noon Saturday.

Saturday dawn came and went. Light came gradually through the top of the tent. Said our Minister: *"This is a new day. Fresh, untouched. What will you do with it?"*

Exactly the question Becky needed to decide.

She was due to open the JFK Library early that morning but the Native American ceremony was in high gear and wouldn't end until noon. Becky knew it could be disruptive to leave early. I told her I would support her either way.

She decided to stay until the ceremony ended at noon. Called the other librarian that was scheduled to be there for her shift, asked her to open the library in her place. Said why she would be late. Done.

The ceremony ended in a powerful way, leaving all of us better than when we had begun the day before. Becky was back at work not long after Saturday noon.

The Head Librarian and her leashed canines were waiting for her. She was fired.

The JFK president was an attorney. He actually knew that the federal law of the time prohibited terminating any employee for attending their religion's event during work hours, much less a Saturday morning. Becky was reinstated. If far from welcome.

Just a week later, a male student working in the library asked her for a date. She said no thanks, but he came back and asked again the same day, twice. She finally said *"No!"* He got the message.

He filed a complaint with HR that her refusal had caused him emotional anguish and ruined his working environment in the library.

The Head Librarian fully supported this charge.

The JFK president drew up some papers for her to sign granting her a generous severance if she would quit her job voluntarily.

Becky was by then very ready to leave. My class was done so I was open to moving on as well.

We both went to the signing.

Before she signed though, the president's attorney handed me my own paper to sign. I wish I still had it. It offered me a thousand dollars if I signed that I would never enter their library again.

Regretfully, I declined. Said that any additional money should go to Becky, since she was the aggrieved party. My paper offer was withdrawn. In this way I missed the opportunity to get $1,000 for a lightbulb.

Asked them to let the Head Librarian know that I might see her in the library soon. Becky added *"Bless her heart. Her little tiny heart."*

Seeing her just in the mythical rear view mirror though. Never went back.

The Candle's Flame

We had left for work at happier job settings but still lived in the vicinity.

Our friend on JFK's faculty, Dr. Yabusaki, had become the president of another university. We both gladly now worked for her.

So when another friend of ours, Ricardo, was hired as faculty at JFK, we went to his welcome ceremony one afternoon.

His friends and family were assembled in a large conference room. On a table in the center was a large unlit candle.

Ricardo thanked us for the celebration. He would begin his new job the following Monday.

He said it was an important part of his culture to thank his ancestors at a beginning like this. The lights were turned down low. Ricardo solemnly lit the candle.

Said the flame was a connection to those who came before. Luck often followed. He began a prayer while we watched respectfully.

Just as the prayer ended, a woman opened the door and entered the conference room. Turned on the overhead lights. Blew out the candle flame.

I knew her! The president's secretary again.

She said to the group *"the president asked me to let you know that the fire code prohibits flame in here!"*

Somebody in the crowd, apparently JFK staff, responded with *"Hey! You and your boss had a birthday cake full of lit candles here on this table just a few hours ago."*

The secretary shrugged and exited quickly.

Ricardo turned off the overhead lights, regarded the unlit candle. Considered lighting it again and then losing his new job before it started.

I just said *"I don't' work here anymore, Ricardo. May I do the honor?"*

Ricardo smiled, stepped back, and waved me in. I lit the candle. Ricardo said a short prayer, was silent a minute with eyes shut. Finally sharing *"the ancestors approve of this new connection. Bad luck will come to those who extinguish the flame. But the message to us who work at this unfortunate place is that we must create our own luck. All here now share that new flame."* Ended the meeting with a final prayer, some good food and cheer.

And Then

You might still want to visit the actual John F. Kennedy Library in Boston. But as to luck for the California JFK University, it was absorbed into National University with only the Law School surviving for long. In the beginning years of the 21ˢᵗ century it all closed completely. Just a whisper of its past existence left in Wikipedia.

Lost in the flame of time.

Spurticus

Theme: *Spartacus* Alex North; *Hot Fun in the City* Sly & the Family Stone

The class of senior women was enjoying exercising in their pool lane.

Until a young male swimmer in the next pool lane stopped each time he came even to splash them, then resumed swimming his laps. Thought it was amusing.

The women caucused. Came up with a joke of their own.

The next time the young man stopped to splash them, they dropped a rubber sperm stress reduction toy named *Spurticus* right behind him.

It followed him in his wake while the ladies cheered and pointed.

All in the pool were laughing with a few taking phone videos.

When he finally realized that he was the center of the joke, he jumped out of the pool, hit the showers.

Spurticus was retrieved for another day.

Those days included holidays.

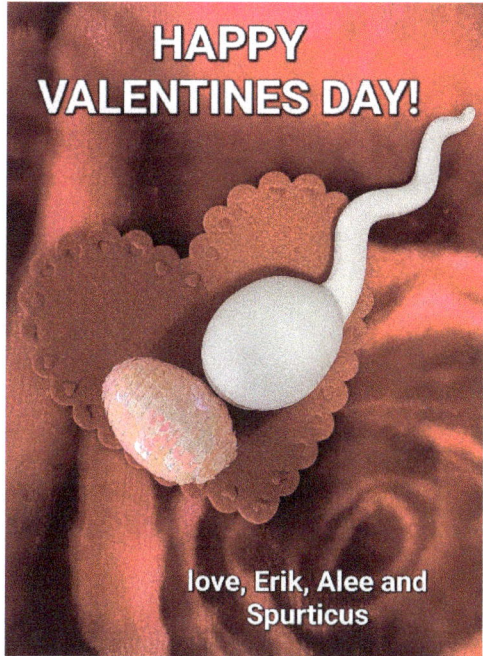

Future Commercial

Theme: *Flight of the bumble bee Violin* Katica Illenyi

The Mosquito Squeezers Blood Bank

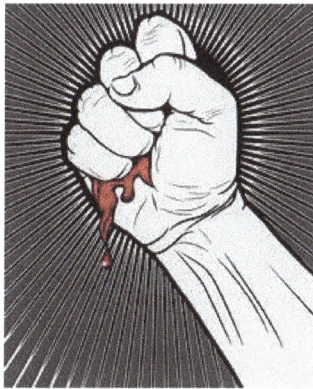

Certified Recycled Purified and Blood Typed

We get back what was rightfully yours!

CONTACT US: The MSBB, Mosquito Island,
British Virgin Islands

Future *Breaking News*

Theme: *Baby, It's Cold Outside* Leon Redbone & Zooey Deschanel

Boeing Starlight Collecting Baby Clothes for Stranded Pregnant Astronaut in Space Station

The planned trip for a few days lasted months into the next year due to dangerous faults in the almost returning Boeing Starlight shuttle. The couple was increasing seen growing more affectionate as the weeks and days rolled on.

Equipment problems for Boeing? Who could have guessed? Asked for comment on how this could have happened, a Boeing spokesperson just spoke their new motto out loud: *"Nobody's Perfect"*.

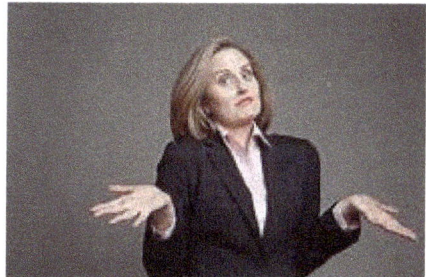

After: Jake Explains Time

Theme: *Great Grandfather* Bo Diddley

1957. Jakob von Uexkull first made me more fully aware of the varying perceptual time world of animals:

> *"Karl Ernst von Baer has made it clear that time is the product of a subject. Time as a succession of moments varies from one Umwelt to another, according to the number of moments experienced by different subjects within the same span of time. A moment is the smallest indivisible time vessel, for it is the expressions of an indivisible elementary sensation, the so-called moment sign. As already stated, the duration of a human moment amounts to 1/18 of a second. Furthermore, the moment is identical for all sense modalities, since all sensations are accompanied by the same moment sign.*
>
> *The human ear does not discriminate eighteen air vibrations in one second, but hears them as one sound. It has been found that eighteen taps applied to the skin within one second are felt as even pressure.*
>
> *Cinematography projects environmental motions onto a screen at their accustomed tempo. The single pictures then follow each other in tiny jerks of 1/18 second.*

If we wish to observe motions too swift for the human eye, we resort to slow-motion photography. This is a technique by which more than eighteen pictures are taken per second, and then projected at a normal tempo. Motor processes are thus extended over a longer span of time, and processes too swift for our human time-tempo (of 18 per second), such as the wing beat of birds and insects, can be made visible. As slow motion photography slows motor processes down, the time contractor speeds them up. If a process is photographed once an hour and then presented at the rate of 1/18 second, it is condensed into a short space of time. In this way, processes too slow for our human tempo, such as the blossoming of a flower, can be brought within the range of our perception.

The question arises whether there are animals whose perceptual time consists of shorter or longer moments than ours, and in whose Umwelt motor processes are consequently enacted more slowly or more quickly than in ours.

The first experiments of this kind were made by a young German scientist. Later, with the collaboration of another, he studied especially the reaction of the fighting fish to its own mirror image. The fighting fish does not recognize its own reflection if is shown him eighteen times per second. It must be presented to the fighting fish at least thirty times per second. A third student trained the fighting fish to snap toward their food if a gray disc was rotated behind it. On the other hand, if a disc with black and white sectors was turned slowly, it acted as a "warning sign," for in this case the fish received a light shock when they approached their food. After this training, if the rotation speed of the black and white disc was gradually increased, the avoiding reactions became more uncertain at a certain speed, and soon thereafter they shifted to the opposite. This did not happen until the black sectors followed each other within 1/50 second. At this speed the black and white signal had become gray. This proves conclusively that in the world of these fish, who feed on fast moving prey, all motor processes – as in the case of slow-motion photography – appear at reduced speed.

A vineyard snail is placed on a rubber ball which, carried by water, slides under it without friction. The snail's shell is held in place by a bracket. Thus the snail, unhampered by its crawling movements, remains in the same place. If a small stick is then moved up to its foot, the snail will climb up on it. If the snail is given one to three taps with the stick each second, it will turn away, but if four or more taps are administered per second, it will begin to climb onto the stick. In the snail's world a rod that oscillates four times per second has become stationary. We may infer from this that the snail's receptor time moves at a tempo of three to four moments per second. As a result, all motor processes in the snail's world occur much faster than in ours. Nor do its own motions seem slower to the snail than ours do to us."

(von Uexkull 1957)

Learning to perceive the *Umwelt* (world view) of animals has the added benefit of enhancing empathy for our own species.

Acknowledgements

Theme: *If I Didn't Care* Inkspots

This 2024 book in the *Time Statues* series has mostly new material. Portions from my earlier books have been modified, or excerpted here. With author permission.

Thanks again first to Asya Blue whose artistry and skills recently completed the 2023 five book *Time Statues Revisited* series, and then the final 2023 *Future Time Statues*. Now, with the next three 2024 books, the final ones in the series, *Time Statue Dreams, Time Statues Harvestt20th Century, and Time Statues Harvest 21st Century,* she and her staff continued essential contributions.

Becky Owl Morgan's carefully thorough editing and counsel was again essential for everything written here. And ongoing encouragement from Tom Hanrahan, Mindy Caruso, Ron Slosky, Angela and Conrad Laran, Stan Krippner, Ann and Ken Yabusaki, and of course Angel Kwanyin Morgan.

Otherwise, pretty much the same as in earlier *Time Statues* work: I thank my past editors from different printing opportunities who encouraged me to write whatever I chose, even if without statistics, graphs, tables, footnotes, or scientific jargon. I was told to just call it *"Commentary"*. Or just write it.

In this I think of Valerie Hearn, with the staff at the *Cambridge University Press*, and Valentine McKay-Riddell, with her staff at the

Four Winds Journal and the *Winds of Change Press*. After decades of publishing about a hundred scientific journal articles and 14 earlier books, it felt good to write the seven time statues books freely and outside the confines of professional custom. I thank colleague Charles Tart who shared his own congruent writing strategy: *'Just write what you really want to say. Then, as needed, you can add any citations, references, footnotes, and anything else an editor suggests.'*

Original material in this series is supplemented with my excerpts and illustrations from the *Four Winds Journal*, the Cambridge University Press *Journal of Tropical Psychology*, the *Bulletin of the International Association of Applied Psychology*: Supplement to *Applied Psychology*: *an International Review, Trauma Psychology in Context: International Vignettes and Applications from a Lifespan Clinical-Community Psychology Perspective, Opportunity's Shadow and the Bee Moth Effect: When Danger Transforms Community, Unfortunate Baby Names,* and the journal *International Psychology*.

As to the key mission of understanding the strange world we live in, and what we can do about it, I thank my Guides. Those include Robert Lee Green, Martin Luther King Jr., David Cheek, Michael Knowles, Rollo May, Nathan Hare, Fred Luskin, Sidney Farber, Robert Dattila, or mentors like Stanley Ratner, Bert Karon, Hans Toch, Lois Fisher, Helga Doblin, Cinnamon Morgan, Canadian-born Angel Morgan, plus the multitudes of my friends, teachers, parents and other relatives (my brother Nelson Morgan and forever sister Pat Norman come to mind, as do her children Elise, James, plus certainly Angela and her husband Conrad Laran). Also Michael Butz, Ben Tong, Ron Slosky, Len Elkind, Ann Yabusaki, and the other thousands of once students in six+ decades of teaching who have taught me much in return.

I have special new appreciation for brilliant editor/inspiration Becky Owl Morgan, Mikael David Owl, guest contributor Angel Morgan, and the relentless motivating encouragement of Dr. Carl Word, Tom Hanrahan, Dorinda Fox, and Dr. Robert Lee Green. Dr. Roland Garcia impressively provided key focused feedback early on for a much improved reorganization. And the example set by my once long lost cousin, the illustrious award winning author Tom Farber.

Respect is due the earlier *Time Statues* reviewers that mixed insight and comment with their own encouragement: Lois Bridges, Valentine McKay Riddell, Theodore Ransaw, Charles Tart, Hans Toch, Ann Yabusaki, with again Nelson Morgan and Robert Lee Green. Great thanks also to Ben Tong for his many contributing illustrations and insightful historical context.

As ever, a thankful appreciation for our recently departed friend Dr. Nathan Hare, founder of university Ethnic Studies in an era *then* while continuation of his contribution is needed *next* more than ever *now*.

Finally, again in continuing memory of Ben Camo, our granddaughter Ava's father:

Octogenarian memory can be tricky. You may be curious about anybody deserving to be acknowledged here that I inadvertently left out. Hope not. But an option we can always use is the answers source we learn about all day long on TV commercials.

Ask your doctor.

"When you sit with a nice girl for two hours, you think it's only a minute. But when you sit on a hot stove for a minute, you think its two hours. That's relativity."
(Albert Einstein, 1954)

Author

Theme: *Time Will Tell (The Wizards)* Susan Anton

Born in the lull between the two world wars, he shares his lifespan perspectives on today's interesting times.

Robert F. Morgan, Ph.D. is a Life Member of the American Psychological Association. An NIMH Pre-Doctoral Fellow at Michigan State University, he continued with more than 50 years of post-doctoral practice and teaching experience. A former speech collaborator and project consultant for organizations including Dr. Martin Luther King Jr.'s SCLC, he was founding editor of the Cambridge University Press *Journal of Tropical Psychology*, and founder of the Division of Applied Gerontology in the International Association of Applied Psychology (IAAP). He has overseen 126 psychology doctoral dissertations in California, Singapore, and Australia, along with a contemporary trauma psychology seminar at the University of New Mexico. He has published more than a hundred articles and 25 books on topics including life span psychology, trauma psychology in context, applied gerontology, international psychology, and even unfortunate baby names. Only semi-retired, he avoids a lethargic status by continuing to think and write. He also hopes to avoid Lincoln's prescient warning: *"It is better to be silent and thought a fool than to open one's mouth and remove all doubt."* Well, his readers will continue to be the judge of that.

Books by Robert F. Morgan

Time Statue Harvest from the 21ˢᵗ Century

Time Statue Harvest from the 20ᵗʰ Century

Time Statue Dreams

Future Time Statues

Time Statues Revisited: Book One: On the Job.

> *Book Two: Language & Influence*

> *Book Three: Citizenship*

> *Book Four: Non-Human Relatives*

> *Book Five: Human Family*

Time Statues

Trauma Psychology in Context: International Vignettes and Applications

Opportunity's Shadow & the Bee Moth Effect: When Danger Transforms Community

Growing Younger: How to Measure & Change Body Age

The Iatrogenics Handbook: Research & Practice in Helping Professions

Training the Time Sense: Hypnotic & Conditioning Approaches

Unfortunate baby names: Slattery's complete collection with the most notable thousands for dramatic and other usage

Electroshock: the Case Against.

Directory of International Consultants in Psychology

Interventions in Applied Gerontology

Measurement of Human Aging in Applied Gerontology

Should the Insanity Defense be Abolished?

Conquest of Aging: Modern Measurement & Intervention

The Effective Verbal Adaptation (EVA) test: Parts A & B

The Educational Status of Children in a District without Public Schools: CRP 3221.

The Educational Status of Children during the First Year Following Four Years of Little or No Schooling: CRP 2498.

Uncas Slattery/the Muddy Chuckle

www.ingramcontent.com/pod-product-compliance
Lightning Source LLC
Chambersburg PA
CBHW051242020426

42333CB00025B/3019